In the Land of
Difficult People

In the Land of Difficult People

24 Timeless Tales Reveal How to Tame Beasts at Work

Terrence L. Gargiulo
and
Gini Graham Scott, Ph.D.

Illustrations by Ron Dias

AMACOM
American Management Association
New York • Atlanta • Brussels • Chicago • Mexico City • San Francisco
Shanghai • Tokyo • Toronto • Washington, D. C.

Special discounts on bulk quantities of AMACOM books are available to corporations, professional associations, and other organizations. For details, contact Special Sales Department, AMACOM, a division of American Management Association, 1601 Broadway, New York, NY 10019. Tel: 212-903-8316. Fax: 212-903-8083.
E-mail: specialsls@amanet.org
Website: www.amacombooks.org/go/specialsales
To view all AMACOM titles go to: www.amacombooks.org

This publication is designed to provide accurate and authoritative information in regard to the subject matter covered. It is sold with the understanding that the publisher is not engaged in rendering legal, accounting, or other professional service. If legal advice or other expert assistance is required, the services of a competent professional person should be sought.

Library of Congress Cataloging-in-Publication Data

Gargiulo, Terrence L., 1968–
    In the land of difficult people : 24 timeless tales reveal how to tame beasts at work / by Terrence L. Gargiulo & Gini Graham Scott.
        p. cm.
    ISBN 978-0-8144-0029-6
    1. Psychology, Industrial. 2. Interpersonal relations. 3. Organizational behavior. 4. Interpersonal communication. 5. Folklore. I. Scott, Gini Graham. II. Title.
    HF5548.8.G34 2008
    650.1'3—dc22   2007045795

Printing number
10 9 8 7 6 5 4 3 2 1

Contents

Preface

Folktales are an entertaining way to deal with the everyday issues that people face in their lives, including how to deal with difficult people in the workplace. Although the tales may be couched in stories about animals and peasants, the types of human characters and behaviors described are universal. They resonate because of their roots in an oral tradition going back to hunting-gathering or agricultural times. Difficult people, then and now, acted out of anger and revenge; were envious and greedy; sought to achieve a better position for themselves and put others down; used lies, misrepresentation, and deceit to gain fortune and protect themselves; and, then as now, gossiped, spreading malicious or embarrassing information to others.

Thus, these stories can also be used to illuminate everyday problems with difficult people in the workplace, as well as suggesting ways to successfully respond, so you don't become a victim of their often dangerous or deceitful ways. To this end, the book is divided into eight sections, featuring the major types of difficult people you may encounter, with three traditional folktales in each section.

Each chapter begins with an introduction discussing the major themes raised in that chapter, followed by three tales about different types of difficult people with those characteristics. Each of these tales is like a warning of what might happen when you deal with such a person. Each tale is followed by advice on how to deal with this type of person.

My coauthor, Terrence Gargiulo, has selected and retold these tales, while I discuss how these tales are reflected in the modern-day workplace, after which I provide advice on what to do when confronted with the type of person described in each tale. In providing this advice, I have made several suggestions. Because every workplace situation is different, you can choose which would be most applicable to your situation. And even if you don't have a particular difficult person to deal with now, you may just enjoy reading these tales and suggestions for advice and fun—and for ideas you can use in the future and to advise others. Historically these tales have been told both for entertainment and to convey a message to apply in one's life.

So enjoy and apply these tales and advice as they apply to your situation. And if you find some special inspiration in using these tales in your own life, please let us know.

—GINI GRAHAM SCOTT

In the Land of
Difficult People

CHAPTER 1

Wicked Wolves and
Other Aggressive Beasts

Introduction

In folktales and fairy tales, the wolf is considered one of the most dangerous beasts. Although it may be crafty like the fox, it is primarily associated with being a ferocious, aggressive, hungry predator out to destroy its prey. One of the most popular classics of the genre is the story of *Little Red Riding Hood*, where the wolf lurks in the forest to find out where Little Red's grandmother is so he can eat her as well as Little Red, and in some versions of the tale he does. Another example is in the story of the *Three Little Pigs*, where the wolf destructively seeks to blow their houses down. Sometimes the wolf is even associated with evil or images of the devil. He (and most always the wolf is a he) is considered wicked, not to be trusted, luring his prey into danger, and then ready to pounce when the prey is most vulnerable. Although the wolf is often a loner, he can become even more dangerous when traveling in a pack with other wolves.

So how do you fight back against the wolf and other such aggressive, dangerous creatures? Generally, in the tales, the victims who survive escape his clutches by getting out of a trap and running away, like Little Red in many of the Red Riding Hood stories; by finding or building a place of refuge strong enough to ward off the predations of the wolf, as did the third little pig who built his home of bricks; or by using some trickery, so the wolf is trapped or killed (as in some of the Little Red stories). But it can be very hard to tame or control the wolf, so it is usually better not to try.

The workplace parallel is the boss who is literally a tyrant and hard to approach about anything. Sometimes a boss may become this way because he is acting defensively from fear, to cut off any resistance and prevent any challenge to authority before an employee raises any questions. It's a way of using command and control, sometimes by rooting out and destroying potential opposition to silence it and stay in command. In some cases these bosses are just naturally aggressive and seek to assert their power. They love the rush that comes from threatening others and keeping everyone in line. And you may also find some coworkers can be this way. They aren't bosses yet, but they act as if they are, and if they *do* take charge, they may be apt to exercise their newly-found power in the same aggressive way, especially when they are new to the position and fearful of any challenges to their authority.

Such bosses — and other workplace wolves — typically like their employees or coworkers to be submissive and deferential, all the better to take advantage of them and get them to do their bidding. And then, at the first sign of a challenge, they are likely to attack. So it's no wonder that they are hard to get along with and are often loners. Like the prowling wolf, they may find it hard to work with other wolf-types as well, since they are all so aggressive. But if they consider you part of their pack, beware: Things may seem fine at first, but when they get angry they may try to push you out.

The following tales illustrate how these wolf-types operate and the best way to deal with them if you find them where you work.

The Wolf and the Goat

(Russia)

Once upon a time there was a goat that built herself a little hut in the woods and lived there with her kids. She often went deep into the forest to look for food, and whenever she left the hut the kids locked the little door and stayed inside. When the goat returned she would knock at the door and sing: "My little baby kids, unlock the door and open it! I, the she-goat, have been in the forest; I have eaten soft grass and drunk spring water. Milk flows down in the udder and from the udder to the hoof and from the hoof into the damp earth." The kids would at once open the door and let their mother in. Then she would feed them and go again into the forest, and the kids would lock the door very tight.

The wolf overhead all this. Once when the goat had gone to the forest he came to the little hut and cried in his rough voice: "Hey, little kids, hey my dear ones, unlock the door and open it! Your mother is back and has brought you milk aplenty." But the kids answered: "We hear you, we hear you, but yours is not our mother's voice! Our mother sings in a soft voice and sings different words." The wolf went away and hid himself. Then the goat came and knocked at the door, singing: "My little baby kids, unlock the door and open it! I, the she-goat, have been in the forest, I have eaten soft grass and drunk spring water. Milk flows down in the udder and from the udder to the hoof and from the hoof into the damp earth." The kids let their mother in and told her that the wolf had come and tried to devour them.

The goat fed them and when she left again for the woods gave them strict orders not to let in anyone who might come to the little hut and beg in a rough voice saying other words than she said. As soon as the goat was gone the wolf ran to the little hut, knocked at the door, and began to chant in a soft voice: "My little baby kids, unlock the door and open it! I, the she-goat, have been in the forest, I have eaten soft grass and drunk spring water. Milk flows down in the udder to the hoof and from the hoof into the damp earth." The kids opened the door and the wolf ran in and ate them all; only one little kid escaped by hiding in the stove.

The goat came back, but no matter how sweetly she sang, no one answered her. She came closer to the door and saw that it was open; she looked into the room and saw that it was empty; she looked into the stove and found one kid there.

When the goat learned of her misfortune, she sat down on a bench, began to weep bitterly, and sang: "Oh, my baby kids, why did you open the door to the wicked wolf? He has devoured you all, and left me with great grief and sadness in my soul." The wolf heard this, came into the hut, and said to the goat: "Ah, neighbor, neighbor, why do you slander me? Would I do such a thing? Let us go to the forest together and take a walk." She replied, "No, neighbor, I have no heart for walking."

"Let us go," the wolf insisted.

They went into the forest and found a pit in which some brigands had recently cooked gruel. There was still some fire left in it. The goat said to the wolf: "Neighbor, let us see which of us can jump across the pit." The wolf tried first, and fell into the hot pit; his belly burst from the heat of the fire, and the kids ran out of it and rushed to their mother. From then on they lived happily, acquired wisdom, and eschewed evil.

Tale-a-Vision

This tale about the wolf and the goats from Russia has parallels with the Little Red Riding Hood story. As the tale indicates, there are two ways to survive an encounter with a wolf: hiding and escaping like the baby kid; or appealing to his pride and getting him to do something that will bring about his destruction, like the mother did.

Similarly, in the workplace, the wolf may be the boss or a coworker, who is out to put down or otherwise hurt the people who work there. Wolf-types show off their power and keep others in place. Too, like the wolf in the story, this kind of boss or coworker might go prowling for information he could use against others, from eavesdropping on conversations to looking at e-mails on someone's computer. Then, just like the wolf used the information from the mother goat to open the door, the dangerous boss or employee will use that information in nefarious ways, such as to damage someone's reputation or to berate or fire an employee who shows resistance or is not submissive enough.

In the folktale, the wolf literally eats up the children. But you can imagine many ways in which a controlling, domineering boss or coworker would figuratively eat up others, such as by draining their creative juices, or killing their motivation and joy of work. Such a person is like a psychic vampire who destroys others who are on the path, particularly if they seem to be in the way. In some cases, when a wolf at work is behaving this way out of fear, he may actually be self-destructive and seeking to take as many victims with him as he can. An example is a paranoid wanna-be film producer, who managed to put together a crew for a film; but then, one by one, she ended up having confrontations with the group. Eventually, people fled, leading to the total demise of the project and with it the wolf's power over everyone in the group.

Take That—What to Do

What should you do if you are dealing with an overly aggressive and controlling wolf-type at work who you feel is threatening to harm you or others? How do you avoid the danger—or possibly turn the tables to get rid of the wolf? Here are some tips. Choose and adapt whatever works best in your own work situation:

- Physically avoid the wolf as much as possible; and shield yourself psychologically. For example, find ways to reduce the amount of time you work together; do what you can without any input from the wolf; and if the wolf tries to brow-beat you, just tune her out.

- Avoid snooping wolves. Lock your drawers and turn off your computer when you leave the office. And provide a wolf-boss with as much information as he needs. That way, he'll have less reason to snoop around.

- Find safe and strategic ways to turn the tables on the wolf. Show her in a bad light to *her* boss, by leaving a door open when she's unjustly yelling at you or a coworker; or by "mistakenly" forwarding a copy of an insulting email.

- If things get bad enough, seek help from someone in authority, such as your boss's boss or someone in HR. They may be able to confront the wolf, putting an end to the abuse and the hostile work environment.

Aniz the Shepherd: An Uygur Folktale
(China)

Once upon a time a landlord hired a shepherd boy whose name was Aniz. He was very well liked. What people liked most of all was to listen to him playing the flute. His flute looked very simple, no more than a length of bamboo, but in his hands it became a wonderful instrument. Whenever they were free, people would sit around Aniz and entertain themselves by listening to him play. The landlord was heartily sick of both the boy and his flute. He was constantly finding fault with him and scolding him, "You little wretch! Do I pay you to sit there playing the flute?" In point of fact, Aniz's flute-playing did not interfere with his sheepherding work in the slightest.

One day the landlord found some reason to give Aniz a beating. That was not enough; he was not content until he had driven him out and trampled his flute into little pieces. "Good! I should like to see you play the flute now!"

Poor Aniz left the landlord's house and, with tears trickling down his face, wandered through the streets. He chanced to meet an old man. "What's the trouble, young fellow? Why are you out here all on your own, crying?"

"I am a shepherd. My name is Aniz. The landlord beat me, drove me out, and trampled my lovely flute to pieces . . ."

"Don't cry, Aniz," said the old man kindly. "Come along and stay with me!" He took Aniz to his home. There he made him a new flute and taught him how to play it. After a few lessons, Aniz could play more beautifully than ever. This time it was not just people who enjoyed his playing; even the animals of the forest came and sat round him. As time passed, Aniz and the animals became close friends.

One day the landlord summoned his sons and said, "Last night I dreamed of a beautiful rabbit, white as snow, with a black spot on the top of its head. You must try your to catch it for me in the forest."

"Father, we have never even heard of such a rabbit!" his sons replied. "Where can we go to catch it for you?"

"You hopeless creatures!" cried the landlord in a temper. "Go and look for it. Whoever finds it will inherit all I have when I die."

The eldest son said "Brothers, let me go! I fear no danger, if only I can make father happy!"

He set off on his way, looking around carefully, and after a while an old man came towards him and asked, "Young man, where are you going?" The eldest son told him why he had come.

"Go to the forest then," said the old man, "and look for the rabbit! Aniz is tending my cattle there. Tell him what you want and he'll help you."

The eldest son went into the forest, found Aniz and asked him for his help. "Of course!" Aniz smiled, "I can help you to find the strange rabbit. But you must bring with you a thousand strings of cash to pay for it."

The eldest son reckoned, "Compared with the property I am going to inherit, a thousand strings of cash are nothing!" He returned to the forest with the money and found Aniz sitting on a tree stump, playing his flute. Animals were squatting round him entranced, pricking up their ears to listen to the music. The eldest son saw the white rabbit with the tiny black spot on the top of its head.

Aniz saw the rabbit too. He put down his flute, stretched out his hand, took hold of it by its long ears and handed it to the eldest son. "Here you are. Hold it tightly! If it escapes, it's none of my business."

The eldest son paid the money, thanked Aniz and set off home with the rabbit. He was about to leave the forest when he heard Aniz playing the flute again. As soon as the rabbit heard the music, it hopped from his hands. The eldest son searched and searched but could not find any trace of it. In the end he gave up and went to see Aniz again.

"The rabbit has run away. What can I do?" he asked.

Aniz answered, "There is nothing I can do about it. I instructed you to hold it tightly. It's no use blaming me."

The eldest son had no alternative but to go home empty-handed and tell his story.

The second son said, "Father, don't worry. I'll go and catch it tomorrow." Next day, the second son went to try his luck and met the same fate as his elder brother. On the third day, the youngest son went, but he fared no better.

It made the landlord very angry to watch his three sons lose three thousand strings of cash like this, without so much as a piece of fluff to show for it.

"You fools!" he cried. "Tomorrow I shall go and catch it myself!"

So the following day he went into the forest. Before the landlord could open his mouth, Aniz took out his flute and began playing. All the wild beasts of the forest came and encircled the landlord. Terror drove the last drop of color from his cheeks. He fell to his knees in despair and entreated Aniz, "Save me!"

"Landlord! Do you remember Aniz? At one sound from my flute, these animals will eat you alive!"

"Don't treat me as once I treated you!" He lay prostrate at Aniz' feet and sobbed, "I promise to give you anything you want. Don't let them eat me."

"Very well. I will spare your life. But you must never bully poor folk again! If you don't turn over a new leaf, I won't be so easy on you next time."

Tale-a-Vision

This tale about the young shepherd Aniz and his landlord is another example of the way a person who has been bullied is able to turn the tables on his tormentor. In this case, however, the tormentor has the opportunity to learn from experience and improve his behavior.

A parallel to this situation is the bully boss, team leader, or coworker who beats people up, not physically, but with his words. Such a person is free with insults and put-downs. He's always ready to find fault in others, but never in himself. He may also be stickler for rules, like the landlord, insisting things be done a certain way even when they could be done another way. Such a person may resent the warm relationships a person develops with others or the times people take to relax and socialize, seeing these as threats to his own power. So even if such socializing and relaxing contributes to good morale, like Aniz playing the flute, it doesn't matter. He wants such activities to stop. If he's the boss, he'll decree it. If he's a coworker without the authority to issue orders, he'll do whatever he can to undermine the goodwill, often by complaining.

Such actions kill motivation. They make employees want to leave or slack off. Yet, there may be hope: Should the bully ever need help from someone with a particular skill, he may suddenly become less of a bully. That's because in such a situation, cajoling and persuasion often work better than bullying. It's a little like what happens with a child who uses a temper tantrum to get what he wants. If the parents ignore him, after a while, when his behavior isn't getting the desired result, he'll stop screaming—and he'll take another approach. He'll try wheedling and begging, appealing to his parents' good nature. This may be a good way to train children not to have temper tantrums. The same approach may also work in the office when bullying doesn't lead the boss or coworker to the desired results and they learn that there is a gentler, more supportive approach to getting a better performance. Then, too, finding support from others can always help, just as Aziz found support from the animals who liked hearing him play.

Take That—What to Do

What should you do if you are dealing with the classic bully, who you feel is threatening you, either verbally or physically? How do you respond to the person who seeks to put you down or is otherwise disrupting office harmony and ruining morale by yelling, by complaining, or by snapping over the slightest resistance or affront? Here are some tips. Choose and adapt whatever works best in your own work situation:

- Show that you have a valuable skill that the bully needs, and use it to negotiate better treatment. Be prepared to withhold your best efforts or your needed skills until the bully treats you better. If you find your efforts and skills are more valued by others, seize

that opportunity and work with those who appreciate you and
treat you well.

- Draw on the support of others when you take a stand against the
  bully. The more power you have — and the more witnesses — the
  more likely the bully will be to back down.

- Once the bully recognizes he needs your help, don't act like a
  bully yourself. It will only lead to resentment and bad feelings
  down the road. Instead, try to show the bully that it's possible
  to get one's way by playing nice. Maybe the bully will try it that
  way in the future.

- Be open to the possibility of helping the bully out in the future
  when he comes to you for help. The bully may learn from his past
  behavior to do better in the future — and you may be well paid
  for your efforts in providing this help.

Tale #3:

Reap What You Sow
(Balkans)

Once upon a time there was a girl named Cveta, who had a wicked stepmother. She and her own daughter slapped and tormented Cveta. The worse they treated her, however, the healthier and prettier Cveta became. One day the stepmother drove Cveta out of the house. "Get out, and don't come back!"

Cveta walked down the road, not knowing where to go. She went deep into the forest and wandered until she saw a fire burning in the distance, where she came upon a little cottage and went inside. The cottage was dirty and in bad need of cleaning. Cveta took a broom and cleaned the cottage nicely. She carried in more wood, and started a fresh fire. Then she sat and waited for the owner of the little cottage to come home.

In the evening, the wind began blowing so hard that the trees snapped as if they had been pulled up at the roots. Shaking with fear, the frightened Cveta hid behind the stove.

Soon a scaly dragoness with enormous wings came flying up. She entered the cottage and began to sniff around. "A spirit sent from heaven is here," she said in a voice surprisingly soft for a dragoness. "Come out, heavenly spirit. I won't harm you."

The trembling girl came out from behind the stove hesitantly. Then the dragoness asked, "Did you clean my cottage and light my fire?"

"I did," Cveta answered.

"Good," said the dragoness. "Now please search in my scales and see if I have any fleas or bugs in my head."

Cveta saw that the dragoness was not the fierce and fiery sort, so she sat down and let her place her head on her lap. To her dismay, she found that the creature's head was full of maggots and smelled like a bug.

"Does my head smell bad, girl?" asked the dragoness.

Cveta did not want to hurt her feelings, so she replied, "No, it doesn't smell bad. It smells just like a bouquet of dried flowers."

Early the next morning, the dragoness went off into the forest. Before leaving, she ordered the girl to feed her animals and to have supper ready for her when she came home in the evening.

Cveta began calling the animals together and began to feed them. When the dragoness came home in the evening, she asked whether her animals had been fed.

"They have," the girl answered.

After Cveta had worked at the cottage for several days, the dragoness took her into a room filled with chests of various colors and shapes. Some were gilded with gold. Others had plain wood veneers. Some were so heavy that they could not be lifted, and others were so small that they could be held in a person's hand.

"If you want, you may go home now," the dragoness said. "Because you have served me so well, you may choose whichever of these chests you like and take it home with you as your reward for helping me so faithfully."

Cveta chose a small, plain chest that could be held in her hand.

"Why have you taken the most ordinary chest?" the dragoness asked.

"Because I know that the least is in it," Cveta answered.

"In the few days that I've been with you, I haven't earned any more than the chest contains."

The unwanted stepdaughter reluctantly started out for home. She was sorry to leave the dragoness that had been kind to her.

When Cveta arrived home with the chest and opened it, she found that it was filled to the brim with golden coins. Her stepmother was impressed.

After listening to the story of her stepdaughter's adventures, she sent her own daughter into the forest to visit the dragoness.

The nasty-tempered girl came upon the same cottage in the depths of the forest. Because she did not want to do any work, she searched for a comfortable nook and fell asleep.

When the dragoness came home in the evening, the wind blew just as the stepsister had warned. The girl was not afraid because she knew that she would not be hurt.

"Heavenly spirit, why haven't you touched my fire or cleaned my cottage?" the dragoness asked.

The unpleasant girl answered, "I don't clean anyone's cottage."

"All right, never mind," said the dragoness. "Please search my scales, and see if there are any fleas or bugs in my head."

The girl peeped into the scales on the dragoness's head and began spitting. "What a stench! I can't stand being near you."

"All right, never mind," the dragoness said.

The next day the dragoness went away into the forest and ordered the girl to feed her animals.

When the girl saw that the animals were wild, she took up a club and began screaming at them and driving all of the animals away.

When the dragoness came home in the evening, she asked the girl whether she had fed the animals. "I fed them all right, with a club — like this!" she said, twirling the heavy club wildly in the air to show what she had done.

"All right, never mind then," the dragoness sighed sadly.

When morning came, she told the girl to go home. "You have served me long enough," she said. "Choose whichever one of these chests you would like and take it home with you."

The girl was delighted to think that she did not have to stay with the dragoness as many days as Cveta had. That's what comes of showing the old bag of scales who's boss, she thought to herself.

She chose the heaviest chest, which was gilded with gold and decorated with jewel-encrusted designs. She nearly broke her back dragging it home. For the first time in her life, she worked so hard that she began to sweat. When she reached home, she and the stepmother quickly opened the beautiful chest. Two terrible green snakes jumped out of it and ate the stepmother and her daughter.

Tale-a-Vision

This tale is one of many, where a goodhearted, kind, helpful person is well rewarded, while someone who is bad-tempered, nasty, and lazy suffers badly in the end. Commonly, in these tales, two or three villains get their comeuppance after the one who helps gets her reward. Often, a stepmother and her daughters are the evildoers — perhaps because they are seen as interlopers in a traditional culture where marriage and lineage are highly valued.

This kind of justice can occur in the workplace when, in response to bad behavior, someone receives the equivalent of a heavy gold chest with deadly snakes inside. Of course, snakes don't *actually* slither out and bite: It may take the form of an office rebellion that unseats a bad boss, or a behind-the-scenes sabotage that prevents the poorly-behaved person from doing their job. For example, on the morning of a big meeting, several employees call in sick, which means that the boss who had mistreated them can't finish his presentation in time. Or a speakerphone is "accidentally" left turned on, broadcasting a boss's yelling fit for all to hear.

Take That—What to Do

What should you do about a person who constantly berates and mistreats others? Should you just wait until their own actions bring them down? How and when can you speed the process along with a little nudge? Here are some tips. Choose and adapt whatever works best in your own work situation:

- Don't take the put-downs personally. Tell yourself, "He's this way with everyone," and remember that his kind of behavior has a way of coming back and biting!

- If possible, disassociate yourself from the bad-natured boss or coworker, so when that person ultimately slips up, she won't drag you down with her. For example, quietly and diplomatically hint at your true feelings to others you trust, so they will know you don't agree with her derisive remarks.

- If problem bosses or coworkers make a poor decision or an error, consider not correcting them. Just let it go. Let them pick the wrong chest, like the mean-spirited stepsister did in the story, and let them deal with the consequences. Obviously, you wouldn't want to use this tactic if it could result in someone getting hurt, or if not speaking up could make you look spiteful.

CHAPTER 2

Cat People and
Other Independent Beasts

Introduction

S tories about individuals who are too independent or set in their ways are another common stable of folktales. In every society, the individual who fits in — "the team player" — is highly valued. Such a person does what is expected, can be counted on to behave, conforms to everyday customs and norms, and acts cooperatively to achieve a goal. By contrast, there are individuals who insist on getting their own way, even when doing so is a mistake. In fact, some individuals may even hang on doggedly to a wrong-headed strategy out of pride, even when they know they are making a mistake.

Some of these tales illustrate the consequences of such behavior when someone behaves this way, thereby providing a "Don't do that" lesson for the contemporary reader or the traditional village, especially its children.

By the same token, these tales can serve as a lesson for the modern office. They illustrate the dangers of being overly inflexible and insisting on getting your own way. Certainly, at times, independence and initiative can be valued. But you have to be aware of when it's appropriate to take initiative and act independently, and when it's appropriate to go along. If you're too independent or stubborn at the wrong times, you may find yourself stepping into traps of your own making. Then, if you continue to assert your independence and refuse help, your pigheadedness will make matters even worse.

The following tales illustrate examples of what happens and what to do when confronted by such a foolhardy and overly independent cat.

Tale #4:

The Cat and the Mice

(Tibet)

Once upon a time there was a cat who lived in a large farmhouse in which there was a great number of mice. For many years the cat found no difficulty in catching as many mice as she wanted to eat, and she lived a very peaceful and pleasant life. But as time passed on she found that she was growing old and infirm, and that it was becoming more and more difficult for her to catch the same number of mice as before. One day, after thinking very carefully about what was the best thing to do, she called all the mice together, and after promising not to touch them, she addressed them as follows:

"Oh! mice," said she, "I have called you together in order to say something to you. The fact is that I have led a very wicked life, and now, in my old age, I repent of having caused you all so much inconvenience and annoyance. So I am going for the future to turn over a new leaf. It is my intention now to give myself up entirely to religious contemplation and no longer to molest you, so henceforth you are at liberty to run about as freely as you will without fear of me. All I ask of you is that twice every day you should all file past me in procession and each one make homage as you pass me by, as a token of your gratitude to me for my kindness."

When the mice heard this they were greatly pleased, for they thought that now, at last, they would be free of all danger from their former enemy, the cat. So they very thankfully promised to fulfill the cat's conditions, and agreed that they would file past her and make a bow twice every day.

So when evening came the cat took her seat on a cushion at one end of the room, and the mice all went by in single file, each one making a profound salaam as it passed.

Now the cunning old cat had arranged this little plan very carefully with an object of her own, for as soon as the procession had passed by with the exception of one little mouse, she suddenly seized that last mouse in her claws without anybody else noticing what had happened, and devoured it at her leisure. And so twice every day, she seized the last mouse of the series, and for a long time lived very comfortably without any trouble at all in catching her mice, and without any of the mice realizing what was happening.

Now it happened that among these mice there were two friends, whose names were Rambé and Ambé, who were very much attached to one another. Now these two were more clever and more cunning than most of the others, and after a few days they noticed that the number of mice in the house seemed to be decreasing very much, in spite of the fact that the cat had promised not to kill any more. So they laid their heads together and arranged a little plan for future processions. They agreed that Rambé was always to walk at the very front of the procession of the mice, and the Ambé was to bring up the rear, and that all the time the procession was passing, Rambé was to call to Ambé, and Ambé to answer Rambé at frequent intervals. So next evening, when the procession started as usual, Rambé marched along in front, and Ambé took up his position last of all.

As soon as Rambé had passed the cushion where the cat was seated and had made his salaam, he called out in a shrill voice, "Where are you, Brother Ambé?"

"Here I am, Brother Rambé," squeaked the other from the rear of the procession.

And so they went on calling out and answering one another until they had all filed past the cat, who had not dared to touch Ambé as long as his brother kept calling to him.

The cat was naturally very much annoyed at having to go hungry that evening, and felt very cross all night. But she thought it was only an accident which had brought the two friends, one in front and one in rear of the procession, and she hoped to make up for her enforced abstinence by finding a particularly fat mouse at the end of the procession next morning. What, then, was her amazement and disgust when she found that on the following morning the very same arrangement had been made, and that Rambé called to Ambé, and Ambé answered Rambé until all the mice had passed her by, and so, for the second time, she was foiled of her meal. However, she disguised her feelings of anger and decided to give the mice one more trial. Thus, in the evening she took her seat as usual on the cushion and waited for the mice to appear.

Meanwhile, Rambé and Ambé had warned the other mice to be on the lookout, and to be ready to take flight the moment the cat showed any appearance of anger. At the appointed time the procession started as usual, and as soon as Rambé had passed the cat he squeaked out, "Where are you, Brother Ambé?"

"Here I am, Brother Rambé," came the shrill voice from the rear.

This was more than the cat could stand. She made a fierce leap right into the middle of the mice. However, they were thoroughly prepared for her, and in an instant they scuttled off in every direction to their holes. And before the cat had time to catch a single one, the room was empty and not a sign of a mouse was to be seen anywhere.

After this the mice were very careful not to put any further trust in the treacherous cat, who soon thereafter died of starvation owing to her being unable to procure any of her customary food. But Rambé and Ambé lived for many years, and were held in high honor and esteem by all the other mice in the community.

Tale-a-Vision

Sometimes a seemingly helpful individual actually has another agenda, and will act to harm others if given the chance. The person may be charming, but can't be trusted. Such a person may claim to have reformed or changed to gain sympathy and trust. Although it is true that some former con artists and criminals do reform and deserve a second chance, others don't. And it can be hard to distinguish the truly repentant from those who are simply angling for another bite at the apple, so to speak. But if you can see through their pretenses, you can prevail.

"The Cat and the Mice" parallels abound in the workplace:

• An employee is on an "action plan" but doesn't actually change. Instead, he manipulates others and gains their sympathy in order to keep his job.

• A boss suggests there will be a big reward after a lot of hard work, and then she invents a last-minute reason to snatch it away.

• An ex-con is hired by the boss as a gesture of goodwill and community support. He blows the opportunity by stealing money or office equipment from the company.

Such people may cover up plans to deceive and thieve by pretending to want to help or by claiming to have reformed from a checkered past. But then, once in a position to do so, they will always take advantage of others, just like the hungry, scheming cat.

Take That—What to Do

So what do you do when you encounter such a devious, deceitful person? And how do you even know whether the person who seems so charming on the surface really is being devious and deceitful? Here are some tips. Choose and adapt whatever works best in your own work situation:

- Be cautious when someone offers to do something out of the ordinary; it may be a genuine offer to help — or there may be a hidden agenda. Monitor the situation as best you can so you can make an informed decision.

- Even if someone new is very charming, be careful when you begin the relationship, whether you are hiring them, agreeing to work on a project with them, loaning them money, or whatever. Check out their references. Think of the beginning of the relationship as a probationary period, and be especially alert.

- Be careful when someone claims to have reformed after doing something very bad in the past. Sure, they may have turned a new leaf, but maybe not. So put your trust on the shelf for a while as you observe them in action, and see if they really have reformed.

Tale #5:

Stubborn Husband

(Asia/Persia)

Once upon a time, a husband had the habit of sitting outside his home every day, while his wife cooked their meals, swept the floor, and washed their clothes. The two quarreled constantly.

"Why do you sit there doing nothing?" the wife asked.

"I am thinking deep thoughts," the husband would reply.

"As deep as a pig's tail is long!" the wife would retort.

The two argued all that morning and all that afternoon. Then, in the evening, the husband and wife both had the same idea at the same time.

"Whoever speaks first," they said simultaneously, "will feed the calf from now on!" The two nodded in agreement, and said nothing more. They went to bed in silence.

The next morning, the wife awoke, lit the fire, cooked breakfast, swept the floor, and washed the clothes. Meanwhile, her husband sat on his bench, smoking his pipe. The wife knew that if she stayed home watching her husband do nothing all day, she would say something. So she went to visit a friend.

A traveling barber passed by and asked the husband if he wanted his beard trimmed. The husband said nothing. "This is my wife's tricks!" the husband fumed. The barber thought he was dealing with a deaf-mute, but he wanted to be helpful, so he trimmed the husband's beard. Then the barber motioned for money. The husband did not move. The barber demanded money again, and became angry. "I will shave off your beard and cut your hair so you look like a woman!" the barber threatened. The husband refused to stir, so the barber shaved off the husband's beard, cut his hair, and left in a huff.

A thief then approached. He mistook the husband for a woman and said, "You should not be out of alone. Have you no husband or brother to look after you?"

The husband almost laughed aloud. "My wife will not give up her tricks!" he said to himself. The thief assumed the husband was a deaf-mute, went into the house, which was filled full of costly carpets, vases, and clothes, and packed everything in a bag. He left with his loot and waved to the husband.

"I will punish my wife for her tricks," the man swore to himself. By then it was midmorning, and the calf in the barn was thirsty. It broke out of its stall, and ran through the village. The wife heard the commotion, and came out from her friend's house. She caught the calf and returned home.

"Who are you?" she demanded, "and where is my husband?

"Aha!" the husband sprang up. "You spoke first, so you must tend the calf from now on!"

The wife was incredulous. "You shaved off your beard." She stormed into house and saw that everything was gone. "What happened?" she demanded of husband. "Who has taken all our things?"

"The man you hired to act like a thief," the husband chortled. "But I did not fall for your deception!"

"I hired nobody!" the wife declared.

"You cannot fool me," the man boasted. "You lost the wager, and so you must tend the calf from now on."

"Foolish man!" the wife exclaimed. "You sat watching a thief steal everything from our house!"

"I knew it was only an act!" the husband gloated.

The wife could barely speak, she was so angry. "You lost your face and your fortune, and all you can think of is our wager!" She glared at her husband, and then said, "You are right, I shall tend the calf from now on. But that is because I am leaving and taking the calf with me. I will not stay with a stubborn fool like you!"

The woman walked to town with the calf and asked a group of children if they had seen a man go by carrying a large bag. The children pointed to the desert. In the distance they could see a man hurrying away, carrying a satchel on his back. She caught up with the thief at an oasis. She sat across from the man, sighing and batting her eyelashes at him.

The thief was flattered by the wife's attention. "Where are you going all by yourself?" he asked her. "Have you no husband or brother to protect you?"

"If I did," the wife said sweetly, "would I be walking in the desert with only a calf for company?"

The wife kept sighing and glancing at the thief, and he soon asked her to marry him. She agreed, and so they planned to stop at the next village and have the chief marry them. By then evening had fallen, and the wife knew it was too late for a marriage ceremony. When they arrived at the village, the chief said as much, and invited them to stay with him for the night.

After everyone fell asleep, the wife arose and looked in the thief's bag. Sure enough, there were all her valuables — carpets, clothes, vases, and money! She loaded the bag on her calf and started to leave. Then she had an idea. She tiptoed into the kitchen, cooked some flour and water over a candle, and poured the dough into the thief's shoes and the shoes of the village chief. Finally she hurried into the desert with her calf.

When dawn came, the thief awoke and found his bride-to-be missing. He looked out a window and saw the woman hurrying away with his sack of loot. He rushed to put on his shoes, but found his feet would not fit in them. The dough in the shoes had hardened like a brick! The thief grabbed the shoes of the village chief, but they, too were ruined. Finally, the thief ran out barefoot. The sun had risen by then, heating the desert sand, and his feet were soon blistered and burned. The thief was forced to halt.

When she arrived at their house, she saw that her husband was not on his bench as usual. She ran inside and found the floor swept, the water drawn, the fire lit, and dinner cooking. But her husband was nowhere inside! She rushed into the courtyard, and there she found him, hanging laundry to dry.

"Stubborn husband," the wife exclaimed, "what are you doing?"

"I lost my face, my fortune, and my wife," the husband replied, "because I was a stubborn fool!"

The wife took the clothes from her husband, and said, "This is woman's work!" At that moment, the calf lowed, demanding water.

"I shall tend to the calf," the husband said.

"No," the wife retorted, "I shall do it." Then the two of them looked at each other and laughed. They came to an agreement, and from that day on, the husband took care of the calf. In the evenings, when they finished their chores, they both sat down on the bench and watched the world go by.

Tale-a-Vision

This tale illustrates what can happen when someone is overly stubborn, insists on taking a particular position, and refuses to back down, even when it leads to negative consequences. The workplace parallel is when someone is overly stubborn and inflexible, resulting in difficulties in accomplishing a task or continuing a valuable relationship. For example, out of habit, pride, or perhaps arrogance, someone insists on performing a task in a particularly inefficient way, resulting in a loss of productivity, equipment breakdown, or even an accident that causes injuries. In business, such stubbornness can result in sticking too long with a poorly-performing ad campaign, manufacturing process, or vendor. In politics, examples abound of the devastation wrought by stubbornly sticking with a foreign policy, monetary strategy, or domestic plan that isn't working.

Unfortunately, it can be hard to reason with such a person when you are not in a position of power. Some, like the husband in the story who only gets it after he loses everything he owns, will learn only after repeatedly finding that their firm, stubborn stand isn't working.

Take That—What to Do

What should you do when you are up against stubborn fools who insist on doing things their way, even when their way isn't working? And what should you do if you don't have the authority to punish or fire the stubborn fool yourself? Here are some tips. Choose and adapt whatever works best in your own work situation:

- Simply let him make whatever mistakes he makes until he comes to his senses.

- Consider whether it really makes sense to continue to stick with him; at a certain point, it may make more sense to simply walk away, so you don't let the stubborn fool's mistakes harm you.

- Try telling him about the consequences of what he's doing. And if that doesn't work, at least you will have done your best to provide a warning.

- Don't take any rejection by the stubborn fool personally; after all, rejecting the wise advice of others in order to do things his own way is part of what makes him tick.

Tale #6:

The Wise Quail

(Jakarta, Indonesia)

One day, a hunter came into the forest. Imitating the quail's own calls, he began to trap unwary birds. There was a wise quail that noticed something was amiss. Calling his flock together, he announced, "My fellow quail, I am afraid that there is a hunter in our forest. Many of our brothers and sisters are missing. We must be alert. Danger is all around us. Listen to my plan. If you hear a whistling call—Twe whee! Twe whee! Twe whee!—as if a brother or sister were calling, be very watchful! If you follow that call, you may find darkness descending upon you.

"Your wings may be pinned so that you cannot fly, and the fear of death may grip your heart. If these things happen, just understand that you have been trapped by the hunter's net and do not give up! Now, this is my plan. You must stick your heads out through webs of the net and, then, you must all flap your wings together. As a group, though you are still bound in the net, you will rise up into the air. Fly to a bush. Let the net drape on the branches of the bush so you can each drop to the ground, and fly away from under the net, this way and that, to freedom. Do you understand? Can you do this?"

"We do understand," answered all the quail as one, "and we will do it!"

Hearing this, the wise quail was content. The next day a group of quail were pecking on the ground when they heard a long whistling call. "Twe whee! Twe whee! Twe whee!" It was the cry of a quail in distress! Off they rushed. Suddenly

darkness descended on them and their wings were pinned.
They had been trapped by the hunter's net. Remembering the
wise quail's words, they did not panic. Sticking their heads out
through the webs of the net they flapped their wings together,
harder and harder and slowly, slowly, with the net still draped
upon them, they rose, as a group, through the air. They flew to
a bush. They dropped down through the bush, leaving the net
hung on the outer branches, then flew away, each in their own
direction, this way and that, to freedom.

The plan had worked! They were safe! They had escaped
from the jaws of death. And, oh, they were happy!

The hunter was not happy. He could not understand how
the quail had escaped him. At last, the hunter realized the truth.
"Why," he said, amazed, "those quail are cooperating! They are
working together! But it can't last. They are only birds, feather-
brains after all. Sooner or later they will argue. And when they
do, I shall have them." And so, he was patient.

Now, the wise quail had had the same thought. Sooner
or later the birds of his flock would begin to argue, and when
that happened they would be lost. So he decided to take them
deeper into the forest, far from their present danger.

That very day something happened to confirm the wise
quail's thought. A quail was pecking on the ground for seeds
when another bird of the flock, descending rapidly, accidentally struck it with its wing-tip. "Hey! Watch it, stupid!" called
the first quail, in anger.

"Stupid is it?" responded the newly-landed quail, flus-
tered because he had been careless, "Why are you so high and
mighty? You were too dumb to move out of my way! Yes, you
were too dumb, you dumb cluck!"

"Dumb cluck is it?" cried the first quail, "Why, talking of dumb, it's clear that you can't even land without slapping someone in the face! If that isn't 'dumb,' I don't know what is! Who taught you to fly anyway—the bats?"

"Bats is it?" yelled the second quail, enraged, "Why, I'll give you a bat, you feathered ninny!" And with a loud chirruping whistle he hurled himself straight at the other quail. An argument had started and, as is the way of arguments, no end was in sight.

The wise quail was nearby and heard it all. At once he knew that danger was again upon them. So he called his flock together and said, "The hunter is here. Let us go elsewhere, deeper into the forest and there, in seclusion, discipline ourselves, practicing our skills. In this way we shall become truly free from the danger."

Many of the birds said, "Though we love our present home, we shall go with you, Wise Quail. The danger is great and we wish to find safety."

But others said, "Why go from this pleasant spot? You yourself, Wise Quail, have taught us all we need to know in order to be free. We know what to do. We just have to stick our heads out, flap our wings together, and fly away. Any dumb cluck can do it! We're going to stay."

So some of the birds flew off with the wise quail, while the others stayed. A few days later, while some of those who stayed were scratching around for their dinner, they heard a whistling call. "Twe whee! Twe whee! Twe whee!" They ran to answer the call when suddenly, darkness descended upon them. Fear gripped their hearts. They were trapped in the hunter's net! But remembering the wise quail's teaching, they stuck their heads through the net, and one bird said, "On the count of three we all flap. Ready? One two, three . . ."

"Hey!" called another bird, "Who made you boss? Who said you could give the orders?"

"I'm the hardest worker and the strongest," said the first bird. "When I flap my wings, the dust rises from the earth and whirls up in clouds. Without me you'd never get this net off the ground. So I give the orders, see?"

"No, I don't see!" shouted another bird. "What you've just described is nothing. Why, when I flap my wings, all the leaves move on the trees, the branches bend and even the trunks sway. That's how strong I am. So if anyone should be giving orders around here it's me!"

"No, me!" shouted a third bird.

"Me!" yelled a fourth.

"No! No! Listen to me!" screamed the first bird again above the rising din. "Flap! Flap! Flap! I tell you. Flap your wings all together when I say 'three!'"

But no one flapped. They just argued and argued. And as they argued, the hunter came along and found them, and their fate, alas, was not a happy one. But the quail who had gone off deeper into the safety of the great forest learned, under the wise quail's guidance, how to really cooperate. They practiced constantly, until they were, indeed, able to work together without anger or argument. Though the hunter tried many times to catch them, he never could. And if he never caught them, why, they're still free today.

Tale-a-Vision

Independence and creativity, while valued traits at times, may lead to disagreements, disputes, and even chaos. Certain situations call for cooperation and team work. It's like that in the workplace, too. When people work together harmoniously, productivity and satisfaction remain high. Everyone pulls together and works toward the same goal. The stakes may not be a literal death like the quail suffered, but disagreements and disputes can lead to the death of a company, a department, or a project. When productivity declines, turnover increases, and costs spiral out of control.

Certainly, a wise quail, whether a boss or a respected employee who effectively takes the lead, can help to bring everyone together to work toward a single goal, so the whole group flies high like migrating birds flying in a "V" formation.. But then when individuals in the group squabble, it takes a strong leader to pull everyone back together.

Unfortunately, not everyone has the authority to pull the arguing quail aside, tell them how to behave, and order them to shape up and fly right. In the absence of leadership, sometimes someone simply has to step up and take the role of a leader. And to help avoid a battle for leadership, it may be a good idea to elect someone from outside the group and authorize that person to provide the needed leadership. If all else fails, consider getting out before the group self-destructs, like the fighting quail trapped in a net!

Take That—What to Do

What should you do when you are caught in a group where others are resisting authority and fighting over who should be in charge, while the situation spirals out of control? What do you do when you don't have the authority of a boss, manager, or supervisor to give the orders to get everyone back into line? Here are some tips. Choose and adapt whatever works best in your own work situation:

- Try appealing to reason by pointing out that the continued arguing is preventing the group from moving forward. But don't try to present yourself as the leader, since the group members may see that as just another attempt to take control.

- If the group can't agree on a single leader, suggest that group members alternate — and propose some kind of lottery system, like drawing straws or rolling the dice — to determine the order in which people take on the leadership role.

- If it appears that the situation can't be fixed and is likely to lead to disaster, find a way to get out before things descend into chaos. Consider transferring to another job within the organization or leaving altogether. Or at least tell someone in authority about what's going on, so they'll recognize your wisdom in understanding the situation. That way, maybe you can save face and gain another job after the rest of the group falls apart and/or others are fired.

CHAPTER 3

Crafty Heroines
Outfoxing Difficult Beasts

Introduction

In folktales, the fox is typically portrayed as a crafty villain, one who suckers his victims — relieving them of their valuables through lies, deceit, and cunning ploys. Similarly, other characters, often rich and powerful, use the qualities of the fox to deceive their poor and humble victims.

But as these heroine tales show, the way to outwit the crafty fox is to best him at his own game by being even more cunning. Trap him in his own lies and stories. Usually in these stories the victim ultimately prevails, showing that these crafty creatures can be outwitted.

These tales provide a lesson that can be helpful for today's employees — or for anyone for that matter who suspects a trick. As the popular saying goes, if something sounds too good to be true, it probably isn't true. Likewise, when someone proposes a bargain that seems especially advantageous to you, there could easily be a catch. Just think of the many real estate and investment schemes where a charismatic sales person makes the offer sound so great that people buy into it, sometimes losing their entire fortunes or savings. Or think of the many cons, where a con artist offers to give you a big share of found money if only you put up a little good faith money yourself. But then the con artist shows no such good faith — and simply runs off with whatever money you put up. And should the police arrive, the con artist is long gone.

So the key to avoiding being taken in is to be aware in the first place and to use your own smarts to counter the bad bargain, as the following tales illustrate.

Tale #7:

The Woodcutter's Daughter

(Central Asia)

There was once a young girl who lived with her father, a wood-cutter. Their home was a tumbledown shack, an axe was the only tool they owned, and a lame old horse and mule were their transport.

The girl's name was Aina-kizz. She was so clever that people came from miles around to ask her advice.

One day the woodcutter loaded his horse with a pile of logs and told the girl, "I am going to market and will be home by dusk. If I sell my logs I'll bring you a little present."

"Be careful, for one man's gain at market is another's loss," she replied.

At the bazaar he stood beside his horse and awaited buyers for his wood. But no one came. As it was getting late, a rich man came strutting through the market. Catching sight of the poor man and his wood-laden horse, he called, "Hey, old fellow, what will you take for your logs?"

"A gold coin, sir."

"Will you sell your wood exactly as it is?" the man asked with a sly grin.

The woodcutter agreed.

"Here's your coin," said the man. "Bring your horse and follow me."

When they came to the man's house, the poor man went to unpack the logs from the horse's back. But the man shouted in his ear, "Stop! I bought the wood 'exactly as it is'—which means the horse belongs to me since it's carrying the wood. If you're not content, we'll go before the judge."

When the judge heard the two complaints, he stroked his beard, glanced at the rich man's silk robe and gave his verdict: The woodman had got his just desserts. It served him right for agreeing to the terms!

The rich man laughed in the woodman's face, and the poor man trudged home to tell his tale to Aina-kizz.

"Never mind, Father, tomorrow I'll go to market," she said. "Who knows, I may be luckier than you."

Next day at dawn she loaded up the mule with logs and, driving it along with her switch, made her way to the bazaar. There she stood beside the mule until the same rich man approached her.

"Hey, girl, what will you take for your wood?" he called. "Two gold coins," she answered.

"And will you trade it exactly as it is?" he said. "Certainly," she replied, "if you pay the money exactly as it is."

"Surely, surely," said the man, holding out his hand to show her two gold coins. "Follow me."

The same thing happened to her as to her father. But she did not mind. As the man smilingly paid her two coins, she said, "Sir, you bought my wood just as it is and you have my mule together with the wood. But you gave your word to pay the price exactly as it is. So now I want your arm as well."

The man was taken aback. His beard shook with rage as he cursed her. But she did not yield. At last, they set off together to the judge. That worthy man heard the complaint, yet this time he could not help the rich man — he had to pay two gold coins for the wood and another fifty for his arm.

How the rich man regretted that he had bought the wood, the horse and the mule. Handing over the money before the judge, he told the girl, "You outwitted me this time, but a sparrow cannot match a hawk. I bet you cannot tell a bigger lie than I can; I'll put five hundred on it. You put the fifty I paid you and whichever lie the judge says is the bigger wins the bet. What do you say?"

"Done," said Aina-kizz.

Winking to the judge, the rich man began his tale.

"One day, before I was born, I found three ears of corn in my pocket and tossed them through the window. Next morning my yard had become a field of corn so thick and tall it took riders ten days to find a way through. And then, by the by, forty of my best goats were lost in the corn. No matter how hard I searched, I could not find them. They had vanished without a trace.

"In late summer, when the corn was ripe, my laborers gathered the harvest in and the flour was ground. Rolls were baked and I ate one, all fresh and hot. And what do you think? Out of my mouth leaped one goat, followed by a second and a third. Then, one by one, out came all forty beasts, bleating hard. How fat they had become — each one bigger than the next!"

When the man fell silent, even the judge sat open-mouthed. But Aina-kizz did not turn a hair.

"Sir," she said, "with such wise men as you, lies can be truly grand. Pray, listen now to my humble tale."

"Once I planted a cotton seed in my garden. And, do you know, the next day a cotton bush had grown right up to the clouds; it cast a shadow as far as three days' journey across the sands. When the cotton was ripe, I picked and cleaned it, and sold it at market. With the money I received I bought forty fine camels, loaded them with silks and bade my brother take the caravan to market.

"Off he went dressed in his best silk robe; but I had no news from him for three whole years. Only the other day did I hear he had been robbed and slain by a black-bearded rich man. I gave up all hope of finding the villain, yet now, by chance, I have discovered him.

"It is you, for you are wearing my brother's best silk robe!"

At these words, the smiles upon the two men's faces quickly dimmed. What was the judge to do? If he said the story was a whopping lie, the rich man would lose five hundred gold coins; that was the bet. Yet if he said she spoke the truth—that was even worse. She would claim compensation for her brother and, besides, for forty fine camels loaded with rich silks.

The man roared like a wounded bull, "You lie, you lie! That's the biggest lie I've ever heard! Take your five hundred gold coins, take my silk robe, and leave me in peace."

With a smile, Aina-kizz counted out the coins, wrapped them in the robe and walked back home.

Tale-a-Vision

The rich man in this tale represents the kind of person who tries to use his cunning to take advantage of others, but who eventually meets his match. In modern terms, this story might remind you of engaging in a lawsuit against a tricky opponent, or in using trickery in the office to stand up to a dishonest boss. Commonly, the employer will prevail if she can define the terms of the agreement, let's say by pointing out that the employee agreed to work until a particular job was completed "to my satisfaction—and I'm not satisfied!" But if the employee can show how "satisfaction" should be defined by a reasonable person's standards, the boss could be presented as unreasonable.

Similarly, the boss who tries to take the credit for an employee's work is using her cunning to take unfair advantage. Perhaps an employee can cleverly take back that credit by casually mentioning something in a meeting about how he enjoyed the boss's great support in working on that project; he might even mention how much the boss was an inspiration in helping him do a good job. That puts the boss in a situation of having to undermine her own contribution to the worker's success in trying to deny the worker's credit for doing the job. In short, such a tricky opponent or boss can be bested if you can cleverly think of a way to turn the tables around.

Take That—What to Do

What should you do when you are up against someone who is like a tricky fox—trying to take something of value from you, whether it's money or property or credit for something you have done? Here are some tips. Choose and adapt whatever works best in your own work situation:

- Carefully review agreements and contracts before you sign them. If you're unclear or suspicious, don't sign, but bring in someone who is more knowledgeable to review the terms.

- If any terms are fuzzy or unclear, clarify them until it is explicit what you are agreeing to.

- Don't feel you have to agree to whatever you are initially offered. You may be able to change or clarify the terms in order to more clearly state what you are agreeing to.

- Be prepared to walk away from any agreement when you feel that the other party is trying to trick you into signing something that will be detrimental to you.

- Remember that when you do sign an unclear, unfair agreement that you may be able to get out of it on the grounds that it is an "unconscionable" agreement created by someone with power over you. You should know that if a court determines that there is uncertainty about what a contract says, the ruling will always go against whichever party wrote the contract.

Tale #8:

The Cruel Creditor and the Judge's Wise Daughter

(Morocco)

In Casablanca there lived a very rich and highly respected merchant, who had an only son. The father died, and before the year was out the merchant's wife and son did not have a single penny. The son had no choice, and he began to beg for alms for himself and for his mother.

The son left Casablanca and settled in Marrakesh. "Who knows me there?" he asked himself. But in Marrakesh there were many rich people, who in the past had done much business with his father and they knew his only son. "Why have you come here?" they asked him.

"I have come to buy goods!" he told them. "But the money that I took with me I spent on the road. If you will lend me money I will return it to you."

One of the rich men said to him: "I can lend you any sum you ask for, but on one condition: You can do whatever you wish with the money and whatever profit you make will be yours. But if at year's end you do not pay up, you must give me two pounds of the flesh of your body."

The unfortunate young man had no choice. He agreed to the condition and signed a contract.

Throughout the year he engaged in business, but he was unlucky. He lost all the money that he had borrowed. Two months before the year's end he stopped taking food because of his anxiety about returning the money on the due late. He was especially worried by the condition that two pounds of flesh would be cut from his body if he did not return the money.

What did the poor young man do? On the seashore there lived a king who had forbidden anyone to enter his palace. Only those who wished to die went there. The young man made his way to this palace, for he could see no other way out. He had not the courage to take his life with his own hands, but he said to himself: "I will go to the palace and there they will kill me."

He wished to enter the palace but, behold, it was shut and bolted. So he went to the window of the king's daughter, and sat there weeping. The king's daughter looked out of the window, but she could not make out who it was below.

Three days passed and he sat beneath the princess' window weeping. On the fourth day the king's daughter called him:

"If you are a man and not a spirit, show yourself and I will do all that you ask, for your tears have touched my heart. But if you are a spirit I cannot help you."

Three times the princess called out to him until he replied. Before he showed himself he asked her to promise that she would not kill him.

The princess promised and the young man emerged from his hiding place. Then the princess saw that he was very handsome. She asked him: "Why do you weep? Perhaps I can help you?"

The unfortunate young man told her who he was, and the princess told him that she had known his dead father.

"I lost all of my father's money. My poor mother has remained at home and who knows whether she has not died already of starvation. I wished to change my fortune and so I changed my place of residence. Then I met a rich man who had known my father . . ." And he continued to tell the king's daughter the tale of his life and of his agreement with the rich man. "Now the time has come for me to return the money, else I must give him two pounds of my flesh."

"Go back to the town of that rich man to whom you owe the money," the princess advised him, "and tell me where you will live. I wish to send you a lawyer in order to help you." The young man remained in the palace and he and the princess loved each other without the king knowing anything of it. Before the year was out the young man returned to Marrakesh. All those who met him asked: "Where have you been all this time?"

And he told them: "I went to such and such a city and there I married the beautiful princess."

"And what about your lawsuit?"

"A lawyer will come and plead the case for me."

The time of the lawsuit came. The princess disguised as a lawyer entered the court. The judge asked the rich man: "What does the young man owe you? What do you want of the young man?"

The rich man took the contract out of his pocket and showed it to the judge. The judge read the contract and asked the young man: "Do you agree that you signed this document?"

"Your Honor! What can I say? You see my signature here. But one thing you must know. I entered into this agreement with the rich man because I had no other choice."

Then the princess rose from her place, dressed in the robes of a lawyer. She addressed the judge: "Your Honor! I agree, on behalf of my client, to give two pounds of flesh to the rich man but I insist that he cut off exactly two pounds. If he cuts off too little then he must make up the difference himself, and if he cuts off too much, he will restore the extra amount from his own flesh."

The rich man rose and said: "I cannot cut exactly two pounds of flesh in a single stroke. I am prepared to waive both the flesh and the money."

When the lawsuit was over, everybody went home. The princess changed her clothes and sought out her husband. "What sort of a lawyer was he that I sent you? Was he an able man?"

"He was very able," the young man replied. "I did not think that I would win the case."

"I will tell you something," she said to him. "I was the lawyer."

The young couple, accompanied by the young man's mother, left Marrakesh where everybody knew him and went to the king's palace. There a brilliant wedding was held, and the young couple lived a life of wealth and happiness.

Tale-a-Vision

This is another classic folktale where a rich powerful person enters into an unfavorable agreement with someone who is poor, vulnerable, and likely to lose. However, the victim is able to prevail by turning the terms of the agreement against the rich powerful person—in this case, with the help of a crafty attorney, who is a woman disguised as a man. In fact, this tale has been so popular that it was turned into a play by Shakespeare, *The Merchant of Venice*.

In terms of today's workplace, the tale illustrates the importance of bringing in effective, wise assistance to help you in confronting a sly adversary — and not readily agreeing to do something the consequences of which may be disastrous. It can be unwise — and unnecessary — to take on a risky venture, like the young man did. After all, he might have had other options, such as working even harder for another merchant or not spending all of the money he earned on the road. It might have taken a little longer to get established, but he could have done so without risking his life. His actions are a little like the go-for-broke speculator who falls for a shady salesman's pitch and invests everything he's got in a fly-by-night scheme. In most cases, he'll lose it all.

People who are cautious and who seek alternatives beforehand don't often find themselves in such a predicament. Yet, if it's already too late — the agreement has been made; the barn door has already been opened, and the horse has escaped — then it becomes critical to find someone who has the knowledge to counter the adversary's own trickery in order to break the agreement.

Take That—What to Do

What should you do when you are faced with a very risky proposition, which promises high losses if you lose? And what should you do when you enter into such an agreement and want to get out of it? Here are some tips. Choose and adapt whatever works best in your own work situation:

- Carefully assess the risks before agreeing to anything; conduct a cost-benefit analysis. Is the potential for failure great and the consequences significant? If so, the risk may be too great. If possible turn down the agreement, try to get out of it, or try to modify it so you have better terms.

- Just because one person offers you an agreement, don't feel that this is the only alternative. You may be able to find someone else who will offer you a fairer deal — or you may not need to take that opportunity in the first place. You may have many other options for a job, for example — you don't have to work in a particular company. You might find another route to get to where you want to go.

- Consider the nature of the person offering to enter into a deal with you. He may be a shady, disreputable character who is trying to take advantage of you, and if you check into his background you'll find he isn't someone with whom you want to be associated.

- In the event you do get stuck in a job or agreement that isn't what you bargained for, look for effective assistance in cutting your losses and getting out of it. For example, if you can show, with some expert help, that you left for good cause, you may qualify for compensation or benefits, rather than be penalized for simply quitting the job.

Tale #9:

The Clever Wife
(China)

A very long time ago there lived in a far corner of China, in Sinkiang, a good and simple man named Fu-hsing, who had an unusually clever wife. All the day long he would run to her with questions and no matter how difficult the problem he took to her, she always thought of a solution. Thanks to her wondrous acumen, the house of Fu-hsing prospered mightily.

Fu-hsing was proud of his wife and often spoke of her as his "Incomparable Wisdom," his "Matchless Wit," or his "Dearest Capability." He only wished that all who passed his house could know it was her cleverness that had brought him such great prosperity. For months he thought about a suitable way of declaring his gratitude, and at last he conceived of a couplet that delicately conveyed his feeling. He inscribed the lines on twin scrolls and posted them on the gate before his house:

"A Matchless Wit like Fu-hsing's
Does with Ease a Million Things."

All who passed the house saw the scrolls, and those who knew Fu-hsing thought what a scrupulous and honest husband he was to thus praise his wife. One day, however, the district magistrate happened to pass that way. On reading the scrolls, he drew his mouth down and his eyebrows together in a terrible frown.

"What a boastful, conceited fellow lives there!" he thought. "What appalling arrogance! Such boasting should not go unpunished!" When he returned to his quarters, he sent a clerk with a stern summons for Fu-hsing to appear before him.

The summons so frightened Fu-hsing that he could scarce speak enough words to tell his wife of it. "I can't understand . . . I'm law-abiding . . . good citizen . . . pay taxes and tariffs without cheating . . ." He pulled at his hair, sprinkling strings of it on the floor. "What have I done to bring upon me this summons?"

His wife laid a calming hand on his before he could tear out the last of his sparse hair. "It must be," she said after a moment's thought, "that the scrolls on the gate have given offense. Really, it is not worth worrying about! Go with the clerk to see the magistrate and have no fear. If you run into difficulty, we can talk it over when you return."

Much relieved, Fu-hsing went off with the clerk and soon was standing before the magistrate, whose eyebrows by now had nudged so close together that they were quite entangled with each other. He sat glowering behind an immense table, his arms folded magisterially into his sleeves.

"So!" he exclaimed. "This is the braggart who posts scrolls on his gate to boast of his extraordinary cleverness!" He leant forward to glare into Fu-hsing's face, the terrible eyebrows bristling like angry hedgehogs. "You would have the world believe you can do anything at all, would you! No matter how difficult?" Loosing his arms from his sleeves, he struck an angry fist on the table. "Very well. I have three small tasks for you to perform. At once! For a fellow of your prodigious talents, they should provide no difficulty. No difficulty whatsoever."

"First, then," and pound went the fist, "you shall weave a cloth as long as a road."

"Second," pound, pound, "you shall make as much wine as there is water in the ocean."

"Third," pound, pound, pound, "you shall raise a pig as big as a mountain."

With a nasty smile, the magistrate uncurled his fist to waggle a long finger under poor Fu-hsing's nose. "Of course, if you do not accomplish these tasks for me one-two-three, you will soon learn how this court deals with swollen heads!"

Wretched and anxious, Fu-hsing hastened home to his wife and stammered out the three impossible demands made by the magistrate.

His wife threw back her head and laughed. "Foolish husband!" she said. "The hardest problems are those with the simplest answers!"

Fu-hsing continued to wring his hands. "But what shall I do? I know that you can accomplish anything, but this is beyond all reason . . ."

Madame Fu-hsing's smile stopped him. "It is really quite simple. Rest well tonight. Tomorrow you must go back to the magistrate and present to him three quite ordinary implements which I shall make ready for you. I will give you certain words to take along with these devices, and you must say them to the magistrate just as I tell them to you."

Fu-hsing attended well to his wife's instructions, and the next morning—carrying a ruler, a large measuring bowl, and a balancing scale—he presented himself to the magistrate once again. When he started speaking, the eyebrows were as tightly knotted as before, but as Fu-hsing continued, and laid in turn the three measuring devices before the magistrate, the brows gradually lifted up and away from his eyes until they became flying birds of astonishment.

"This morning, as I was setting out to do the tasks you gave me," Fu-hsing began, "I realized that I needed further instruction from you before I could finish. Therefore, your Honor, I have taken the liberty of bringing these three measures to facilitate your task. I must respectfully ask you, first, to measure the road with this ruler that I may know the length of the cloth I must weave; second, measure the ocean's water with this bowl that I may know how much wine I must make; and third, weigh the mountain with this balance that I may know how big a pig I must raise." Fu-hsing made a deferential bow. "Just as soon as you have set the standards, your Honor, I shall be pleased to finish the tasks."

So confounded was the magistrate at the cunning solution to his three problems that he allowed Fu-hsing to go without punishment, and never ventured to bother him again. Truly, the magistrate believed Fu-hsing's Matchless Wit could do a million things.

Tale-a-Vision

This tale is a cautionary tale about the dangers of being too boastful or arrogant (although here the character manages to overcome a difficult challenge with the help of his clever wife). This is a longstanding cautionary tale in many societies, because harmony and good relations depend on cooperation. When one person seeks to stand above others, this can breed jealousy and envy that frays the bonds of society. This principle is true even in the United States. Though it's an achievement-oriented society that values individual success, once someone becomes extremely successful, it often triggers envy and criticism. There is an ongoing tradition in popular literature about how someone who has been very successful is brought down to size by a personal flaw or tragedy.

There's no shortage of workplace parallels here, such as when an employee brags too much or too loudly about her success on or off the job. Although other employees may initially want to praise her and complement and honor her for the achievement, she must show some humility and tact in accepting that praise. Otherwise, the other employees who once bestowed their praise may become resentful. They may feel she has become too arrogant, too big for her britches, just like the magistrate felt about Fu-hsing. And then they may want to bring the boastful employee down to size, such as by testing her knowledge with tasks she can't do or questions she can't answer. But then, maybe, with a little help from an assistant or mentor, she may be able to show herself to be worthy, and that the praise was justified, even if she went a little too far in showing off after an achievement.

Take That—What to Do

What should you do when you feel you have been very successful at achieving something, but don't want to appear arrogant by gloating about your success? How do you keep others from viewing you as difficult because you seem too much of a show-off? Here are some tips. Choose and adapt whatever works best in your own work situation:

- Let the honors for your achievements come from others, rather than singing your own praises.

- When people praise you, be gracious and humble; don't use the occasion as an opportunity to gloat and crow about how great, accomplished, and successful you are.

- When you are praised for an accomplishment, think about how you can praise others who contributed to your success. By sharing the praise, others are better able to feel a part of your success and will be less likely to resent you for an achievement that elevates you above them. By making them part of your success, you elevate them as well. This helps to promote good feelings and loyalty to you, rather than a desire to challenge you and show you up.

- If you have had an assistant or mentor who has contributed to your success, honor that person publicly. Others will recognize that you are generous, rather than arrogant—that you do not keep the honor and glory all for yourself.

- When you are challenged, consider inviting an expert to help answer any questions put to you. And be sure to acknowledge those who help you in these challenges. After all, you may need them again to assist you in the future. If you acknowledge their help now, you will be more likely to get it later.

CHAPTER 4

Lions and Other Power-Hungry Beasts

Introduction

In the office bestiary, lions and other aggressive creatures are the most dangerous and power-hungry animals. It is their nature to be ferocious, and they like to show it off.

Such beasts are common subjects of countless folktales. Often, their comeuppance is at the hands of the smaller and cleverer heroes. In these tales, the abuse of power often leads to the overly aggressive character's punishment or demise. You might call it justice or karma. Again and again, malicious and vicious behavior leads to bad consequences in these tales. Perhaps it's because the heroes tend to be the common people, or smaller and cleverer animals. After all, these tales are told by and for everyday people. So the overly aggressive animals are like evil and exploitive kings, queens, landlords, and warlords.

In the office — and in modern life generally — justice or karma works like that, too. If you know how to deal with the aggressive and dangerous "beasts" in your own life, not only are you more likely to survive and thrive, but you may even become the hero of a modern-day tale about besting an aggressive beast who preys on the weak!

In the following chapter, you'll meet some of these beasts who are eager to attack at the slightest opportunity. But then you'll learn ways to counter or avoid such attacks altogether.

Tale #10:

The Lion and the Hare

(Persia)

There once was a beautiful meadow, which was the home of many wild animals. The animals would have lived there quite happily had it not been for one mischief-loving lion. Every day this lion wandered about, killing many helpless creatures merely for the sport of the slaying. To put an end to this, the animals gathered in a body, and approaching the lion, spoke to him in this manner:

"King Lion, we are proud to have such a brave and valiant beast to rule over us. But we do not think that it is fitting for one of your rank to hunt for his own food. We therefore wait upon you with this request: Henceforth, if you remain quietly at home, we your subjects will bring to your lair such food as it is fitting that a king should eat."

The lion, who was greatly flattered, immediately accepted their offer. Thus, every day the animals drew lots to decide who among their number should offer himself for the lion's daily portion. In due time it came about that the lot fell upon the hare. Now the hare, when he learned that it was his turn to die, complained bitterly.

"Do you not see that we are still tormented by that lion?" he asked the other animals. "Only leave it to me, and I will release you for all time from his tyranny."

The other animals were only too glad at these words, and told the hare to go on his way. The hare hid for some time in the bushes, and then hurried to the lion's lair. By this time the lion was as angry as he was hungry. He was snarling, and lashing his yellow tail on the ground. When he saw the hare, he called out loudly:

"Who are you, and what are my subjects doing? I have had no morsel of food today!"

The hare asked the lion to calm his anger and listen to him.

"The lot fell today," he began, "on another hare and myself. In good season we were on our way here to offer ourselves for your dinner, when a lion sprang out of the bushes and seized my companion. In vain I cried to him that we were destined for the King's table, and moreover, that no one was permitted to hunt in these royal woods except your Majesty. He paid no heed to my words except to retort, 'You do not know what you are saying. I am the only king here. That other lion, to whom you all bow down, is a usurper.' Dumb with fright, I jumped into the nearest bush."

The lion grew more and more indignant as he listened to the hare's tale.

"If I could once find that lion," he roared, "I would soon teach him who is king of these woods."

"If your Majesty will trust me," answered the hare, humbly, "I can take you to his hiding-place."

So the hare and the lion went out together. They crossed the woods and the meadow, and came to an ancient well, which was full of clear, deep water.

"Yonder is the home of your enemy," whispered the hare, pointing to the well. "If you go near enough, you can see him. But," he added, "perhaps you had better wait until he comes out before you attack him."

These words only made the lion more indignant. "He shall not live a moment after I have laid eyes upon him," he growled.

So the hare and the lion stealthily approached the well. As they bent over the edge and looked down into the clear water, they saw themselves reflected there. The lion, thinking that it was the other lion with the other hare, leaped into the well, never to come out again.

Tale-a-Vision

The lion in this story is the perfect example of the neighborhood bully who torments and tyrannizes everyone with his strength, but has little smarts. Though he flashes his stuff to remind everyone how all-powerful he is, he can easily be outwitted. When challenged by a cleverer creature, his power quickly disappears, since he has no wisdom or common sense to back it up.

In the office setting, this can translate into a domineering boss who rules with the proverbial "iron fist," but who is highly vulnerable because employees don't trust her. In fact, they may be eager to show their anger and resentment when she isn't looking. Commonly, this translates into poor performance, high turnover, and absenteeism. Some employees, like the little hare, may go a step further, using their wits in a quiet, unobtrusive way to harm the aggressive boss. Or if this blowhard is a coworker, another employee might easily put him in his place. Call it backstabbing, sniping, or pulling out the rug—the upshot is that the overly aggressive boss or coworker goes down—sometimes even permanently.

For example, an employee in the role of the hare might leave a phone off the hook or a door ajar, so others can hear or see the boss or coworker in an embarrassing or compromising situation, which could be job death in a corporation. An employee might let the boss take the wrong turn on the way to an all-important meeting. A coworker might trick a rude, insulting coworker into saying something insulting to an important visiting client. Just use your imagination to think of all the things someone who might feel like playing the hare might do to a power-hungry boss or coworker! But be careful before you actually take any vengeful actions yourself, since they might backfire if you get discovered, or someone could get seriously hurt.

Although certain actions might be fine — like reporting a boss's bad behavior to a supervisor or HR — in other cases you may just want to imagine yourself taking these actions, so you feel somewhat better. In this exercise — sometimes called "mental revenge" — you imagine all the things that would give you a sense of justice; you might even share your feelings with a trusted coworker. But don't act on these feelings! That way you won't get in trouble and no one will get hurt.

If the no-nothing bully is a customer or client, you might refuse to provide further services. Then, if the service is one the customers or clients sorely need and can't get elsewhere except at a much higher cost, they have in effect fallen into the pool of water like the lion.

Take That—What to Do

What should you do if you encounter a lion who's acting aggressively and is full of his or her own power, but doesn't seem to know which end is up? Here are some tips. Choose and adapt whatever works best in your own work situation:

- Just go along to get along and let the lions make their own mistakes; eventually they'll fall into a trap.

- Get out of the boss's or coworker's way when they're on a rampage. Avoid them until they calm down; for example, take a break or go out to lunch.

- Quietly and strategically point out the boorish behavior to others. And if you can find others you trust who feel similarly, invite them to do the same so that higher-ups will get the message.

- If there's a supportive manager above your boss or coworker, report what's going on (preferably as part of a group). Then, someone with even more power may help put the burly boss or coworker in a cage where they belong. (Though use this approach judiciously, since it can backfire if the higher level boss or owner isn't supportive and sees you as a complainer; you have to be sure of your facts and are reporting a serious case of misbehavior by your boss, as well as choose a strategic way to do this – such as by setting up a private meeting or going with a group to show the problem is pervasive. And it's also good to come with a suggestion for what to do about the situation that will improve morale and productivity in the office.)

- Politely tell a super-aggressive client or customer that you sincerely regret not being able to serve them satisfactorily — and then don't serve them any more

The Nobleman and His Cook

(Hungary)

There was a nobleman in Hungary, who was so much in love with his cook that he would never ever eat anywhere else except at home. But as much as he was pleased with her cooking, he was just as much displeased with her temper. Because she really had a vicious temper.

Every once in a while, at the slightest provocation, or even without provocation, she would just start banging around the pots and pans and the lids and would simply declare that today she was not going to cook "and you can go out and eat in the restaurant and catch an indigestion!"

Moreover, she would even threaten to leave him, leave him for good. So the poor nobleman, being so much in love with her cooking, lived in a constant fear of losing her, and with that the delicious meals she used to prepare for him.

Well, this life went on for years, and it wore him out quite a bit, so one day he simply decided that he was going to put an end to her constant threats and tricks, and tie her down so she simply wouldn't be able to get away from him, and would be forced to cook for him.

Of course, he could do this only in one way: by marrying her. And after that, of course, she wouldn't be able to say to him, "Well, I'm not going to cook today," or "I'm going to leave you." The loyal wife would be forced to obey him and cook his meals and that's all there was to it!

So to the great amazement of his other wealthy colleagues (many of them were members in the Hungarian parliament) he married her, willing to face even social ostracism for the sake of a good meal!

Well, after the wedding day, as usual, he went out to perform his duties, and afterwards rushed back, thinking, "Ah, now at least I will find a peaceful home and good food on the table."

He came home, and behold, the stove was unlit, no food on the table. So he went to his wife and said, "Well, what about the food? Didn't you cook today?"

And what did she say? "Would you, the son of a noble family, permit your own wife to do the cooking? From now on I'm through with cooking for good, and if you want to eat, you better hire us a cook!"

Tale-a-Vision

The message here is that when people's roles and relationships change, or when someone moves up the social or career ladder, so do their expectations — and you may need to adjust your expectations as well.

This folktale presents the common story of someone in a lower class being able to move up into a higher class as a result of a special skill or attribute that appeals to someone in a higher class. It's the same story that is told in the classic Cinderella fairy tale, where a woman who has been turned into a scullery maid by her stepmother and stepsisters so entrances the prince that he falls in love with her, and after he finds her, he makes her his queen. So now she becomes fully privy to the luxurious life of nobility and she leaves her life of servitude behind. (In fact, there is no expectation that she should continue to clean and serve her stepmother and sisters as before, though in the classic tale, she graciously arranges for her stepmother to have an apartment in the castle and for her stepsisters to marry wealthy nobles.)

The same dynamic occurs in the workplace. As people move up the ladder, they have higher expectations of having more power, respect, and responsibilities associated with the new position. Therefore, their relationships with others can and should be expected to change. It would be nice if everyone were sensitive and flexible enough to adjust the way they treat people who have arrived at a new and higher status; some, however, will need a nudge in the right direction.

At times when it is strategically appropriate, the employee might mention other potential offers—just like the cook spoke about leaving—while noting that she has turned down the offers to remain with the company. This way she shows she would like to stay, but there is a potential for a more responsible job elsewhere from someone who recognizes her value. It's a way of highlighting the valuable skill that the current employer won't want to lose.

Upon being promoted, an employee may need to demonstrate or remind others — diplomatically, of course — of her new status requiring different behaviors. For instance, after being promoted to a manager, an employee who used to get the coffee or run errands for other managers might, if asked, say she isn't doing that any more and suggest another employee who might take over that task. Another example may be a newly promoted manager no longer going out "with the boys" or "with the girls" after work.

At the same time, an employer in the role of the noble should recognize that once he promotes an employee to a new position, he should not expect that employee to continue to perform tasks that aren't normally part of the new role. He should recognize that the promoted employee will have raised expectations for how others will treat her in the new status, and the boss should take the lead in treating her appropriately. In fact, the boss should provide a model for this new behavior for the rest of the workplace, so others will understand how to treat the newly-promoted employee. As a result, there will be clearer expectations for everyone and less chance the newly promoted employee will feel resentful or frustrated if others continue to treat her as they did before her promotion.

Take That—What to Do

What should you do when you are trying to work your way up into a higher status position or have just been promoted into one, but the person in power isn't giving you the proper respect or is expecting you to continue to do the tasks associated with your old position? Here are some tips. Choose and adapt whatever works best in your own work situation:

- Make sure your boss recognizes the value of your talent or skill by, for example, discreetly pointing out how you contributed to a particular project.

- If you feel your boss doesn't appreciate your talent or skill, find a strategic time to mention how others have valued it, how you might have other opportunities, but that you really do want to stay. This involves some risk. If you do it, be prepared for your boss to "call your bluff" and tell you to go ahead and pursue the other opportunities.

- Exude the confidence and assurance that goes with your higher-status position, so you can confidently say "no" to tasks that are now beneath your new role.

Tale #12:

Thodora

(Greece)

Once there were two kings who ruled neighboring kingdoms. One of the kings was rich and strong and had great military power. This king had a son who was known in every kingdom for his kindness and bravery.

The other king had a smaller kingdom and was less powerful. This king had three daughters. The two kings lived in peace, until one day the stronger king put it in his mind to claim his neighbor's kingdom and unite it with his own.

And so the more powerful king sent a message to his neighbor warning him to surrender willingly if he wanted to keep some of his power and his riches. If he refused the offer, his entire family would become slaves.

As soon as he received the bad news, the less powerful king got up from his golden chair and moved to the bronze chair to muse over the situation. You see, this king had three chairs: a golden one for when he was happy, a silver one for when he was calm, and a bronze one for resolving difficulties. Seeing her father sitting on the bronze chair, his older daughter came to him.

"What is it, my father?" she asked. "What's bothering you that you are sitting in the chair of worry?"

"A great misfortune has fallen on our kingdom, Daughter," he told her. And he went on to explain their neighbor's decree.

"Do we have a choice, Father?" she asked. "We know our neighbor is stronger and that he can easily conquer us. You should surrender without a war. Do you want to make slaves of us?"

"I will never surrender," the father replied. "Even if I have to sell everything to build an army, I am determined to resist our enemy."

"Have you no concern for us, Father?" she cried out. "Shouldn't you be thinking of our dowries? Shouldn't you be thinking of marrying us to the best young men in the country rather than sacrificing us?"

When she saw that her father could not be persuaded, the oldest princess stormed out of the room.

In a while, the second daughter came to her father. This daughter was also worried about her father, but when she heard of his plan, she too became angry and left him to himself.

Soon afterward the youngest daughter, whose name was Thodora, came to her father. She too was concerned to see her father distressed.

When the father tried to explain what a terrible dilemma was torturing him, Thodora interrupted him. "Say no more, Father," she cried. "We will never surrender our country to the enemy! But why make war when war brings so much misfortune to people? Couldn't this conflict between the two kingdoms be resolved in a duel?"

"Of course," the king said, "but how? Our neighbor the king and I are too old for a duel, and I have no son to challenge our neighbor's son."

"But you have me, Father," the young princess said. "I will disguise myself as a man and defend our kingdom and honor. From now on, you can call me Thodoris."

At first, the king would not hear of it, but the princess was so determined to save her country that the king finally gave in and agreed to her plan.

At once he sent a message to his neighbor the king to suggest that they settle their dispute in a duel with swords. Whoever won would get both kingdoms.

To this, the other king agreed, of course, for there was no one in the world that could match his son's bravery.

When Thodora was ready to set off for the duel, her father gave her his blessing. At that very moment, a dog mysteriously appeared in front of Thodora. This dog was visible only to her. Then Thodora mounted her horse, and with the dog behind her, rode off to the neighboring kingdom. The king and his men followed.

Both young people fought fearlessly. But with her dog's encouragement, Thodora finally managed to catch the prince off guard and wound him. The prince fell to the ground, his pride more hurt than his body.

Soon thereafter, Thodora and her men took over the enemy's palace and settled there. Thodora was more anxious to see the young prince heal than she was to claim the kingdom she had won. Every day Thodora visited the wounded prince, and soon a warm friendship developed between the two. It did not take long before Thodora fell in love with the prince. And the prince? He could not understand his attraction to his enemy. Soon the suspicion that Thodora was in fact a woman became fixed in his mind. The prince went to his mother and revealed his suspicions.

"A girl at war! This is unheard of!" his mother said. "But if you must, take your friend to the woods and sleep there for a night. When you wake up, check the places where you both slept. If your side remains cool and his dries up, then your friend must be a woman. At least, that's what people say."

Now, the dog heard this conversation and warned Thodora of the prince's scheme. When the two young people went to the woods to spend the night there, the girl waited for the prince to fall asleep. When he did, the girl moved from her spot near him and slept somewhere nearby. Just before dawn, she returned to her place near the prince. When they awoke, the prince checked the places, and saw that his friend's place was cooler than his own.

"See what a big mistake you have made?" said the queen when her son told her what had happened. "Now there is no doubt that your friend is a man."

But that very night, Thodora decided to leave the palace and return home. She could no longer play this game. Before leaving, she wrote a note:

"Thodora I came and Thodora I leave. But I leave a winner."

In the morning, when the prince found the note, he put it to his heart, leaped on his horse, and rode off like the wind to Thodora's kingdom. All the people in both kingdoms rejoiced over the young couple's reunion.

Tale-a-Vision

This folktale is a perfect example of why there is no reason to give in to the outrageous demands of someone who seems more powerful. The expectation, of course, is that someone who is less powerful, like the second king with a smaller kingdom, would rather surrender than lose it all. This kind of give-up-and-give-in-so-I-won't-attack-you scenario has many parallels, from Hitler's easy take-over of Czechoslovakia before World War II to the local mob boss rolling up to a mom-and-pop store in New Jersey or Queens. Then there is also the neighborhood bully who terrorizes the smaller and younger kids at school and demands that they give up their lunch money, or else he will beat them up.

But by using one's wits and cunning, one can defeat such bullies. It may not be possible to have a direct confrontation between opponents, since the big bully may be too powerful, as was the case in the fable, where the rich and strong king with the large kingdom was too big for the king with the smaller kingdom to take on in battle. But there can be alternatives, as shown by Thodora's posing as a man and fighting the king's son.

A parallel in the business world is a large company telling a smaller one, "Sell to us on our terms or we'll destroy you," or a real estate developer trying to frighten small property owners into selling at a low price. On the illicit side of business, consider an organized criminal gang that "provides protection" to store owners by extorting money lest the stores mysteriously catch fire in the middle of the night.

Yet there are ways to fight back, and often the little guy does prevail. One common strategy is to raise public sympathy by taking the story to the media or by gaining help from a wise mentor—much like Thodora got help from a little dog. Or in some cases, like a property owner who refuses to sell to the developer, it may help to bring in a lawyer. Often the media will pick up on such a David vs. Goliath tale, and public opinion will force the developer to back down. Then, again, maybe the bully has a weak spot—a fear or a skeleton in his closet. Or he could be subject to a higher authority he fears, such as his boss, or perhaps even the law! In short, if you can't win by confronting oppressive behavior directly, you may be able to succeed in a round-about way using your wits.

Take That—What to Do

What should you do when you encounter a bully who is trying to coerce you into giving up something valuable? To paraphrase an old proverb, "All's fair in love, war, and bully-battling." Here are some tips. Choose and adapt whatever works best in your own work situation:

- Look for the bully's weak spot and see if you can attack there.

- Try using some subterfuge or deception to maneuver the bully toward self-destruction. Consider how you might use a behind-the-scene strategy to undermine the bully so he ultimately fails—never knowing who undermined him.

- Look to others for advice or intelligence that will help you succeed in defeating the bully.

- Don't think you have to stand up to the bully directly; you can win some decisive battles by sitting down and using your wits.

- Sometimes it helps to let bullies think you are going along; then catch them off-guard and beat them with your wit, the help of others, or both.

CHAPTER 5

Snails and Other Lazy, Unwilling-to-Commit Beasts

Introduction

Have you worked with people who are lazy or unwilling to make the effort to do something? Or they make promises but don't follow through? Or perhaps you have encountered people who are unwilling to make a commitment. They say they need time to make a decision, but then they dillydally, and never get around to finally deciding—or if they do, their decision is too late.

Such people are snails—the lazy, take-it-slow slackers who would rather relax than get things done. If you wait for them to act, you may grow very frustrated. You want them to move at your pace, but they move at their own. You want them to act, but their usual response is inaction—or delayed action, and incomplete at that. It's as though they are listening to their own inner drummer, and they keep listening, without ever actually marching. They're in their own little world, which is comfortable for them. They are resistant to change or anything that shakes things up. Plus, in the comfort of their little world, they don't care much for what others think or do, except as it affects them. Even when they talk about changing, they probably will just talk and not actually change, because snails like lazing around, doing things slowly.

Unfortunately, there are lots of snails around, and you often find them in the same kinds of locations, where there isn't much movement. That's because at the first sign that things are going to be shaken up, the snails are sure to disappear. After all, it's so much more comfortable back in their little shell. So as a general rule, you can't expect too much from a snail, which means that if you have a lot of snails around, not much will get done. So what should you do about snails? You should get a few ideas from the following tales.

Tale #13:

The Snail and the Rosebush

(Denmark)

Around the garden ran a hedge of hazelnut bushes, and beyond it lay fields and meadows with cows and sheep. In the middle of the garden stood a blooming rosebush, and under it sat a snail, who had a lot inside its shell — namely, himself.

"Wait till my time comes," it said. "I'll do a great deal more than grow roses, or bear nuts, or give milk, like cows and the sheep!"

"I expect a great deal from you," said the rosebush. "May I dare ask when this is going to happen?"

"I'll take my time," said the snail. "You're always in such a hurry! That does not arouse expectations!"

Next year the snail lay in almost the same spot, in the sunshine beneath the rosebush, which was budding and bearing roses as fresh and as new as ever. And the snail crept halfway out of its shell, stretched out its horns, and drew them back in again.

"Everything looks just as it did last year. No progress at all; the rosebush sticks to its roses, and that's as far as it gets."

The summer passed; the autumn came. The rosebush still bore buds and roses till the snow fell. The weather became raw and wet, and the rosebush bent down toward the ground. The snail crept into the ground.

Then a new year began, and the roses came out again, and the snail did, too.

"You're an old rosebush now," the snail said. "You must hurry up and die, because you've given the world all that's in you. Whether it has meant anything is a question that I haven't had time to think about, but this much is clear enough — you've done nothing at all for your inner development, or you would certainly have produced something else. How can you answer that? You'll soon be nothing but a stick. Can you understand what I'm saying?"

"You frighten me!" said the rosebush. "I never thought about that at all."

"No, you have never taken the trouble to think of anything. Have you ever considered yourself, why you bloomed, and how it happens, why just in that way and in no other?"

"No," said the rosebush. "I was just happy to blossom because I couldn't do anything else. The sun was warm and the air so refreshing. I drank of the clear dew and the strong rain; I breathed, I lived. A power rose in me from out of the earth, and a strength came down from up above. I felt an increasing happiness, always new, always great, so I had to blossom over and over again. That was my life; I couldn't do anything else."

"You have led a very easy life," said the snail.

"Certainly. Everything was given to me," said the rosebush. "But still more was granted to you. You're one of those with a deep, thoughtful nature, one of those highly gifted minds that will astonish the world."

"I've no intention of doing anything of the sort!" said the snail. "The world means nothing to me. What do I have to do with the world? I have enough to do with myself and within myself."

"But shouldn't all of us on earth give the best we have to others and offer whatever is in our power? Yes, I've only been

able to give roses. But you? You who are so richly gifted—what have you given to the world? What do you intend to give?"

"What have I given? What do I intend to give? I spit at the world. It's no good! It has nothing to do with me. Keep giving your roses; that's all you can do! Let the hazel bush bear nuts, let the cows and sheep give milk. They each have their public; but I have mine inside myself. I retire within myself, and there I shall stay. The world means nothing to me." And so the snail withdrew into his house and closed up the entrance behind him.

"That's so sad," said the rosebush. "I can't creep into myself, no matter how much I want to; I must go on bearing roses. Their petals fall off and are blown away by the wind, although once I saw one of the roses laid in a mother's hymnbook, and one of my own roses was placed on the breast of a lovely young girl, and another was kissed by a child in the first happiness of life. It did me good; it was a true blessing. Those are my recollections—my life!"

So the rosebush bloomed on in innocence, and the snail loafed in his house—the world meant nothing to him.

Tale-a-Vision

The snail in this tale is the classic example of the thinker and dreamer who imagines all kinds of possibilities for the future, but then does nothing to make it happen. Action is always sometime in the future, because the snail isn't ready to act. Unfortunately, the snail is paired with a rosebush, who is like the stick-in-the mud person who acts, but does the same thing year after year and can't do anything to change the snail. While the snail is only concerned about himself, the rosebush wants to help others, but this help is limited, because the rosebush can only produce roses. The rosebush and snail are stuck in a kind of co-dependent relationship, where the snail does nothing, and the rosebush isn't able to change the snail's behavior in any way; it continues to support the snail doing nothing, while the rosebush does the same thing year after year.

In the workplace, you are more likely to find the snails working in loner jobs — computer operators and numbers crunchers — though they might turn up in other positions. But wherever they are, it's just in their nature not to be very good at working with other people, and they are slow to get anything done. In fact, they may have a "What's in it for me?" attitude when asked to do any extra work. And they're unlikely to volunteer for anything. They'd rather slack off and take the extra time for themselves than contribute the best they can. Meanwhile, the rosebushes in the office would prefer to look the other way rather than confront the snail about why it isn't doing more or relating well to others in the office.

It's a situation that will continue for a long time unless someone intervenes. You may not want to shake up the rosebushes, since these are the good, steady workers whom you can count on to bloom — that is, to produce — week after week, month after month, year after year. But you do need to get the snails moving and acting, or else they'll drain your resources. Alternatively, you may need to get rid of the snails. Not only are they unproductive, because they are so slow or don't act to complete a task, but their ideas would be hard to implement, because the ideas are unrealistic. And they don't work well with others, thereby undermining morale.

Take That—What to Do

What should you do when you are confronted by a snail in the workplace? What if you lack the authority to punish or fire the snail yourself? Here are some tips. Choose and adapt whatever works best in your own work situation:

- Since the snail is a loner who doesn't like working with others, it is best to put the employee in a position where he can work on his own. Or, if you are a coworker, try to interact with the snail as little as possible; pick up any work the employee has done when it's finished, and don't try to make any small talk.

- Since the snail is slow and lethargic about getting work done, give him plenty of time to complete the work and try giving earlier-than-necessary deadlines so that, hopefully, he'll turn in his work on time.

- If the snail complains about other people or life in general, don't take it personally; avoid listening, tell him you're busy doing something else. He may eventually get the picture that you don't want to hear his incessant griping.

- Try to get the snail to come out of her shell, so she will be less isolated and have more energy without that protective shell to lug around. For example, gradually give her more responsibilities involving interaction with others, and bestow plenty of praise and reward as encouragement for each achievement. Sometimes snails curl up in their shells because they fear getting hurt if they come out. They may even dream of emerging from their shells, and with each small success, they may be more willing to come out a little more.

- And if all else fails, give the snail an ultimatum: "Either speed up and become more productive, or you're out of the garden!"

Tale #14:

The Tatema

(Mexico)

At six o'clock in the morning Mario was fast asleep. And he was still asleep at seven, at eight, at nine, at ten. Usually Mario would wake up about eleven. Then he would ask his wife to go to the store to get tortillas and coffee for his breakfast.

Fortunately for Mario, the storekeeper was a childhood friend of his and never asked him to pay for his food. But one morning the storekeeper woke and said to himself: "Why should I work so hard, getting up at five every morning, while my friend lies in bed all day enjoying himself? No. He will have to help me before I give him any more food."

That morning when Mario's wife arrived at the store, the storekeeper refused to give her any food. "Tell your husband that I'm building an extra room on my house and I want him to help me carry some large rocks from the quarry. After he helps me, then you can come for the food."

"Oh no!" said Mario, when he heard what the store-keeper had said. "Those rocks are much too heavy for me to move. How many times must I say: 'If God wishes to give, He will give, even if He has to push it in through the window?' Please, no more talk of work." With that, he dressed and left the house.

Mario was walking up the hill and watching the clouds drift across the sky, when suddenly he heard shouts behind him.

"Whoa! WHOO-AA!"

Turning around, he saw a runaway horse, heedless of his rider's cries, charging up the path.

"WHOO-AA WHOA!" the rider cried again, but the horse paid no attention.

Just as the animal raced by, Mario leaped forward without a thought for himself, grabbed the bit, and brought the horse to a halt.

Mario held the reins while the rider dismounted. The rider was an old man with a long white beard.

"You are both wise and brave," he said to Mario. "You do not run here and there like the others, but when the moment is important, then you are there. You risked your life for me today and I want to reward you by giving you a tatema."

Mario looked puzzled.

"A tatema is a gift given by God to man," the old gentleman explained, "and only the man God gives it to may keep it."

He motioned for Mario to follow him and they continued up the hill. Then the gentleman stopped and pointed to a large flat rock. "Underneath that rock," he said, "are oak leaves. Under the oak leaves are wooden chests. If you open the chests you will find the tatema waiting for you."

Mario bent down and pushed aside the rock. He brushed aside the leaves, and there were six wooden chests. Slowly he opened one of the chests. It was filled with silver coins. He opened a second chest. It too was filled with silver coins. He opened a third . . . all six chests were filled with silver! Mario turned around to thank the old gentleman, but he and his horse were gone.

Mario scooped up a handful of coins and put them in his pocket. Then he closed all six chests, covered them with leaves, and put back the rock. By now he was exhausted. He sat down under a tree to rest and fell asleep.

When Mario woke up, it was late in the afternoon and he

was hungry. As he hurried down the hill for his supper he heard a clinking noise. He stopped. The noise stopped. He started on again and the clinking began again. Then he put his hand in his pocket and brought out . . . six silver coins.

When Mario's wife put the coins in the storekeeper's hands, she said: "My husband sends you these. We need rice, beans, a chicken, tortillas, tomatoes, and coffee."

The storekeeper looked at the silver coins in amazement. "How did Mario get so much money?" he wondered aloud.

"Come to our house tomorrow," the wife said, "and he will tell you."

The next afternoon the storekeeper heard the whole story.

"But, Mario," he asked, "why didn't you bring the chests home with you?"

"Oh, they were much too heavy," Mario said. "I would need mules to carry them and I have no mules. Anyway, by now, dear friend, you should know: If God wishes to give, He will give, even if He has to push it in through the window."

"I have mules," the storekeeper said. "I will come to your house tonight and we will go to the rock together. If you give me three of the chests, my mules will carry all six down the hill. What do you say?"

"Fine," said Mario.

The storekeeper returned to his store. But the whole rest of the day he kept thinking to himself: "Why should I divide the treasure with Mario? After all, it is I who own the mules. He will never own mules. He would never even know what to do with his share of the money. Whereas I, I shall buy more mules, build a larger house . . ."

That night at eleven o'clock Mario was sound asleep.

"Husband," said his wife. "Wake up. It is past eleven and your friend has not come."

"Oh, he's just late," said Mario and he fell back asleep.

An hour later the wife woke her husband again.

"Husband, wake up! It's midnight and I'm afraid your friend has decided to keep all the silver for himself."

"Midnight? So late? It's much too late to go anywhere now. Wife, come to sleep."

So the wife lay down and she and Mario both slept soundly through the night.

Meanwhile the storekeeper had arrived at the flat rock with his mules and his servants. He ordered the servants to remove the rock and look under the leaves. They did so and found the six wooden chests. "Open them quickly!" the storekeeper said. But when the servants opened them, they saw the chests were filled, not with silver, but with foul-smelling mud.

"My friend has tricked me!" the storekeeper cried. "Well, I will trick him right back!" He ordered his servants to load the chests onto the mules, to carry them down the hill, and to dump all the mud in front of Mario's house. They did this and rode away.

The next morning when Mario's wife woke up, she could not open the door. She tried the wooden window, but it too was stuck.

"Husband, wake up," she said. "There is something outside our house and we are trapped inside."

Mario got out of bed, and he pushed on the window while she pushed on the door. Then he pushed on the door while she pushed on the window. She pushed and pushed and pushed, and at last the window opened a crack. A shower of silver coins fell onto the floor.

"Husband," the wife said, "your friend came after all!"

Later that morning the wife went to the store and ordered not only food, but new clothes for herself and Mario. Before the storekeeper could question her, she put down on the counter twenty silver coins and said:

"How kind you have been to us! We waited last night until midnight and I was afraid you had changed your mind. But then this morning the coins came pouring in through the window. Surely you gave us more than half."

"No, no," the storekeeper protested. "It wasn't me."

"Of course it was you. Who else would have left all those silver coins outside our house?"

There was silence in the store.

Then the storekeeper said quietly, "Your husband has already told us: If God wishes to give, He will give . . . even if He has to push it in through the window."

Tale-a-Vision

In this tale, Mario is the lazy-but-good-natured dreamer who does as little as possible, while counting on outside help to get by. It can be infuriating to deal with such a person. He routinely turns down requests to help out because it would be too hard or time-consuming. But then, sometimes—like the little kid who wishes for and ultimately gets that special Christmas present—in the nick of time he gets just what he needs. It seems miraculous! Someone must be looking out for him. Despite his laziness, he is rewarded, perhaps because when it really mattered he spontaneously came to the aid of another person. And of course because he is good na-tured, he shares his fortune with his friends and loved ones.

Take That—What to Do

What should you do about a good-hearted but lazy person who may do great things occasionally, but more often slacks off? What if you don't have the authority to discipline or fire this person yourself? Here are some tips. Choose and adapt whatever works best in your own work situation:

- Try appealing to his better nature. Consider him like a diamond in the rough, which just needs a little polishing up to really shine. For example, praise him, tell him how important doing some-thing is, and maybe, just like Mario, he will save the day.

- Give him your support or the support of others to help him achieve a task; he may need that extra push to take action. And then reward him as you promised for doing the work, even if you had to provide that extra push and backup.

- Find out what he wants so you can motivate him to do what you want. Maybe it's more money, like the silver coins that motivate Mario to go to the rock, or the desire to help others that was trig-gered when he saved the man on the runaway horse. Once you have a good idea of how to motivate the Mario in your work-place, you can use those motivators to get him to perform.

- Be prepared for the person to do a great job sometimes and slack off at other times. Consider assigning him to less urgent jobs, autonomous teams, or special projects without critical deadlines so he can slack off at times but still do quality work. For example, consider assigning him creative tasks in a skunk works project. Under the right conditions, given enough time, and with a little luck, he could come up with a million ideas — a few of which may even be great ideas. If not, well, at least he won't interfere with critical operations.

Tale #15:

Hannah and Mother Ocean

(Unknown)

Hannah lived with her aunt in a small hut by the sea. Every day she gathered sea shells to sell at the town's market. Hannah's day was always the same. In the morning with a song in her heart, Hannah danced and frolicked with the waves as she collected shells of every shape and size. Without fail Mother Ocean bestowed Hannah with a colorful basket of shells. In the afternoon under the relentless sun, Hannah sold her treasures at the market, and then at night she returned home to give her aunt the money she had earned.

After a sparse meal, Hannah's aunt counted the coins and placed them in large jar. She always said, "Hannah, you're a sweet girl, your mother would be proud of you. If you work one more day, I'll probably be able to afford to send you to school."

But every day was the same and Hannah began to lose heart. As time passed Hannah could think of little else other than her wish to go to school.

One morning Mother Ocean called out to Hannah and said, "Dear child, your heart grows darker every day. What sadness is consuming you? Tell Mother Ocean what's troubling you and I'll see how I can help you."

"Oh, Mother Ocean, I long to go to school to play and learn like all the other children in the town. My aunt has promised me that as soon as we have enough money she will send me to school, but every day she says the same thing and nothing new ever happens."

"I see," said Mother Ocean. "When you come to see me

tomorrow bring me your aunt's brush, her sash, and a pair of her shoes."

The next morning Hannah placed her aunt's brush, sash, and pair of shoes in her basket and went to see Mother Ocean. Mother Ocean instructed Hannah to bury the objects in the sand. When she was done Mother Ocean gave Hannah half the number of shells she ordinarily did. Then Mother Ocean said to Hannah, "Your aunt will wonder why you are bringing her fewer coins. You must tell her that I'm concerned about your family's well-being and that I would like to help her."

Hannah did as Mother Ocean had asked her. Her aunt was very intrigued by Mother Ocean's offer and promised Hannah she'd go with her in the morning to see Mother Ocean. When morning came Hannah went to wake up her aunt, but her aunt just rolled over in bed and told Hannah to go to the beach by herself.

That morning Mother Ocean had even fewer shells for Hannah. She cautioned Hannah, "Your aunt will be upset that you are bringing fewer coins home and she will tell you she spent the whole day looking for her brush. Ask her to come see me tomorrow morning. Promise her I'll give her a brush finer than the one she's lost."

When Hannah gave her aunt the coins, her aunt was upset and threatened, "If you don't bring home more coins you'll never go to school." Then Hannah's aunt started to complain how she spent the whole day looking for her brush but it was nowhere to be found. Hannah told her aunt to come with her in the morning to accept Mother Ocean's gift of a new brush. Hannah's aunt was pleased and agreed to go with Hannah in the morning.

But when morning came and Hannah went to wake up her aunt, her aunt just rolled over in bed and told Hannah to go to the beach by herself.

That morning Mother Ocean had even fewer shells for Hannah. She cautioned Hannah, "Your aunt will be upset that you are bringing fewer coins home and she will tell you she spent the whole day searching for her sash. Ask her to come see me tomorrow morning. Promise her I'll give her a sash more beautiful than the one she has lost."

Later, when Hannah gave her aunt the coins, the aunt was upset and threatened, "If you don't bring home more coins you'll never go to school." Then Hannah's aunt started to complain how she spent the whole day looking for her sash, but it was nowhere to be found. Hannah told her aunt to come with her in the morning to accept Mother Ocean's gift of a new sash. Hannah's aunt resisted, saying: "If I cannot brush my hair, it blows wild in the wind. How can I go out in the morning?" After Hannah assured her aunt that Mother Ocean had a special sash, she seemed pleased and agreed to go.

But when morning came and Hannah went to wake up her aunt, her aunt just rolled over in bed and told her to go to the beach by herself.

Mother Ocean was beside herself. "Why does your aunt refuse to honor my request? Doesn't she know about my great generosity?" So Mother Ocean gave Hannah even fewer shells and warned her, "Your aunt will be upset that you are bringing fewer coins home. She'll tell you she spent the whole day looking for her shoes. Ask her to come see me tomorrow morning. Promise her I will give her new shoes that never wear out."

When Hannah gave her aunt the coins, the aunt screamed,

"Wretched girl! I swear you will never go to school. Now help me find my pair of shoes or I will give you a whipping."

Hannah implored her, "Mother Ocean wants to give you a new pair of shoes, which will never wear out."

Hannah's aunt chased her out of the house with a broomstick: "Bring me more coins or never come back."

Grief stricken, Hannah ran to the beach in tears. Mother Ocean heard Hannah's cries and soothed her with warm waves to tickle her ankles. Then she said, "Don't be afraid, Hannah. Go to where you buried your aunt's brush, sash, and pair of shoes."

Hannah did as Mother Ocean instructed and to her great surprise saw a huge overflowing pot of gold coins. Then she heard Mother Ocean say, "Promise me, dear child, that you'll flee from here and go to another town where you can go to school."

Tale-a-Vision

Another type of difficult person is the type who makes promises but doesn't follow through, even when it is in his own best interest. Most of the time, this person is either too lazy and doesn't care, or he made the promise to placate the other person, but never meant to honor it. Bottom line: You just can't trust this person to keep his word.

Hannah's aunt is like the employee who slacks off at work but wants more money, who doesn't keep his promises, and who always finds plenty of excuses for not getting his job done. Or she is like a vendor or contractor who agrees to complete an assignment by a certain date, but part-way through, asks for more money. Such individuals are not only lazy and greedy, but can't be trusted.

Take That—What to Do

What should you do about a lazy, greedy, and untrustworthy employee, vendor, or contractor — especially if you lack the authority to discipline him or show him to the door? Here are some tips. Choose and adapt whatever works best in your own work situation:

- Meet privately with the person. Share your concerns and see if he's willing to change. If so, offer to provide the assistance.

- If the employee is unwilling to discuss the situation, it may be time to say goodbye (if that's an option), because you don't want to work with someone you can't trust.

- Give the employee an opportunity to change by entering into a contract for change, specifying exactly what you want changed — for example, Don't be so lazy, Be realistic in your expectations, or Do a certain task or series of tasks. If the employee changes, fine; if not, it's time (once again, only if you're in a position to do so) to let that person go.

- If you don't have the authority to fire, have a private discussion about your concerns. Suggest that you would like to come up with a way that you can work together better. If the person is willing to make changes, that's great. If not, do what you can to avoid having to work with him in the future, or at least reduce the amount of time you spend together.

• If another employee is really dragging down the group morale by his lazy, greedy, and untrustworthy ways, talk to others in the group. If you are all agreed, go as a group to your boss. Air your concerns and let the boss, HR, or the company owner handle it.

CHAPTER 6

Ravens and Other Untrustworthy Tricksters

Introduction

S ome difficult people can be very charming on the surface. They are seemingly friendly and helpful, sometimes even seen as heroes and revered for the good they do. But in reality they may be self-absorbed, scheming, ready to spread gossip, and determined to destroy anyone who gets in their way. They are like the tricksters in many mythologies and folktales who may be thought of as heroes for their cleverness, but who are actually more like con artists. Sometimes they get away with their chicanery; at other times they are exposed and ensnared by their own recklessness.

You may consider such characters as being difficult because they are playing dual roles. On the one hand, they are such suave, cool individuals that you want to work with them. You may feel such a warm connection that you are willing to share information, even confidential information, because you feel you have developed such a strong bond of trust. But then you get caught in a sucker's game, because they are really self-centered, self-interested characters, most concerned with what's in it for them, rather than doing what's right. At heart, they are ethical pragmatists, most interested in what works, in what they can get away with when the opportunity presents itself. So, at the first chance they get, they will pounce on the opportunity or spread your secrets. As the following stories illustrate, they simply can't be trusted; they will act in their own interest and against yours.

So what should you do when you are dealing with either a boss or an employee who is a charmer, but who in reality is an untrustworthy trickster? The following stories will give you some insights into the many types of devious tricksters you may encounter — and what to do about them.

Tale #16:

The Winter Raven

(Native American)

Winter raged with fierce howling winds through the forest and every tree shook with fear. No end was in sight and all the animals were suffering greatly. Although it had never been done before, Owl decided to call a special meeting of all the animals to discuss the situation.

Owl assumed his perch on an old tree with wide branches. He used his great strong wings to shield himself from the freezing wind. All the animals from the forest both large and small gathered around a fire built by the badgers and squirrels. Never one to miss any action, Raven flew to one of the highest branches of a pine tree and scornfully watched the proceedings of the meetings. Most of the animals did their best to avoid Raven whenever they could.

Owl began in a voice true and solemn: "As you know, my dear brothers and sisters, winter will not be kind to us this year. Unless we can devise a plan on how to help each other many of us stand to die. What do you think we should we do?"

When Owl's question was met with silence, Raven began to laugh in a loud voice at all the animals.

A small mouse ventured forward and with eyes full of fear said, "I have food stored for my family — it is not much but I will share what I have."

At this Raven laughed so loud he almost fell off of his branch.

Then a family of hares hopped forward, "We too have food stored away in our burrows. We will share whatever we can."

Owl was moved by the generosity of these humble animals and said, "This is a start, not an end to our problem, but perhaps others of us have food we can share."

Then the coyotes and wolves came forward and said, "We do not have any food stored, but when there are breaks in the heavy snows, we'll go to the nearby farms and get chickens, eggs, and whatever else we can find."

Raven cackled, "You are the most treacherous and selfish animals here. You will only take for yourselves and care nothing for anyone else." Then Raven screamed at the other animals, "How can any of you believe such nonsense? Even when you are hungry, don't you have more sense than this?"

Then the deer stepped forward and said, "We will go with the coyotes and wolves. They can put the food on our backs. Together we can bring enough food back for all of us."

When the deer had finished Owl gave a reassuring look to a young group of owls who declared, "We'll serve as lookouts. We can fly ahead of the coyotes, wolves, and deer to make sure they're not in danger of being caught."

All the bats of the forest nodded in eager agreement and shouted, "We'll help the owls."

Raven shook his head in disgust. This was the craziest thing he had ever heard. Without a second thought he jumped down to the ground and began kicking dirt over the fire while beating his wings in a jeering dance. He mocked all the animals in haughty voice singing, "No one will survive. No one will survive. You must fend for yourself. Nothing will save you from winter except your own abilities to survive. I'll have nothing to do with these plans. I'm free to fly and find a place away from this wretched winter and free from your stupidity."

The cloud of dust kicked up by Raven was so big that Raven

could not see where he was going. Before anyone could try to stop him, he stepped right in the heart of the fire and went up in a column of flames.

That is why in the winter, when you are cold and hungry and you're warming yourself by a fire, look off into the distance where the fire casts its shadows and you'll see Raven still dancing.

Tale-a-Vision

While the raven plays many roles in Native American literary — from a clever cultural hero and creator to a scheming, ever-hungry bird, here he is the self-interested individual who doesn't want to share and cooperate like the rest. And ultimately he is destroyed by his own selfishness, which sometimes happens to the individual who goes his own way and doesn't want to be a part of the team.

The message for the workplace is the importance of teamwork. Certainly, there may be some people who feel more comfortable working alone, and they may do a good job completing independent tasks. But generally, people need to be able to work together to do a good job and for productivity to remain high for the organization as a whole. The need to work together can be especially true when there are stressful situations, such as a difficult deadline to meet, which is like the hard winter the animals face in this story. That's when team members may have to make some sacrifices to complete the task, such as working late, forgoing a weekend trip, or changing a vacation to another time. Then, if the whole team pulls together, the group will be able to complete the task successfully.

But someone like Raven could possibly derail the group effort. For example, he might dampen everyone's spirit; he might persuade some people whose work is crucial for the group not to put in the extra effort, causing the group to fail.

Or perhaps the naysayer might simply point out how the project is not worth doing, how it's a waste of effort, and how it's likely to fail. But if the team members are able to ignore his negative input, like the animals in the tale ignored Raven, they can do well, while putting the naysayer in his place. So, in effect, the naysayer's influence goes up in flames, like Raven.

Take That—What to Do

What should you do if you encounter such a person who discourages teamwork or disparages the team's efforts? Here are some tips. Choose and adapt whatever works best in your own work situation:

- Don't listen to the naysayer who urges non-cooperation. If no one on the team listens to her, her negativity will have no influence and will not be able to disrupt the work.

- As a group, tell the naysayer to get lost. Explain that if she wants to work independently that's fine, but that the rest of you want to work together without her interference.

- Report the naysayer to your boss or manager and explain how her input is undermining the group's morale and its ability to work together. Then, the boss or manager will likely talk to the naysayer, put her in her place, or even fire her for insubordination or other actions that threaten to undermine the group.

- Invite the naysayer to join the group and explain how it will be beneficial to work together. Then, if she is still uncooperative and antagonistic, use one of the above strategies — ignore her, tell her to get lost and work on her own, or report her to your boss or manager.

Tale #17:

The Iron Chest

(France)

Once upon a time there was a poor peasant. One morning before sunrise he rode into the forest to cut wood. There, under an oak tree, he met a very old woman. She was standing before a large iron chest, and she said to him, "You can redeem me and make yourself lucky! This iron chest is filled to the top with gold coins. Take it home with you, but tell no one a solitary word about it or it will bring you misfortune."

The man was delighted to hear these words. He loaded the chest onto his wagon, thanked the old woman and rode back home.

As the wagon pulled up to the door he said, "I'm not supposed to tell anyone, but you are my dear wife, so the promise I made doesn't apply to you."

"That's right," said the peasant's wife with curiosity. "I'll be as silent as the grave. What is it then? Why are you coming home so early from the woods?"

"That's exactly what it is!" answered the peasant. "I found a large chest full of money under an oak tree. We shall never want again. But be sure to hold your tongue."

With that they lifted the chest from the wagon and carried it into the cellar. Then the peasant's wife took a gold coin out of the iron chest, bought some meat, and roasted it on the hearth. What joy! However, her neighbor had hardly smelled the delicious odor when she hurried over, sniffed, and said, "What are you cooking?"

"Oh, neighbor," replied the woman, "I can't tell anyone,

but of course you can keep a secret. When my husband was driving into the forest to cut wood, he found a large iron chest full of money beneath an oak tree."

"That is wonderful," said the neighbor. "You told the right person, for I won't repeat it to a soul!" Then she ran back to her house.

Not long afterward her brother's wife came to visit her from the neighboring farm. "Sister-in-law, do you know what has happened?" she asked her. "But you must be able to hold your tongue!"

"Oh, as though I were a blabbermouth!"

"I know, and that's why I said that. Our neighbor from over there, the little peasant, while he was cutting wood in the forest he found a large chest of gold under an oak tree."

The sister-in-law didn't indeed hold her tongue and instead carried the story to the sexton's wife, and before the sun went down the story had found its way to the magistrate. He summoned the peasant before him and said, "I know it all! You stole a chest of money, and it is in your cellar. Turn over the money!"

"No, my lord," answered the peasant. "That is not true. I am as poor as a church mouse and am an honest fellow. I've stolen nothing."

"That will be determined, old friend," replied the magistrate. "Your wife herself said so."

"Oh, my lord, my wife is crazy."

"Go now! The court meets in two weeks. At that time we will see if your wife is crazy."

The peasant did not feel well as he left the magistrate's estate, and he thought of the words the old woman had spoken to him under the oak tree. But he did not lose courage. He hurried home, took a handful of gold coins out of the chest, hitched up his wagon, and drove into town. There he bought all the bread rolls that the bakers had in stock, so that he had dozens of bushels to load into his wagon. He drove back home and scattered the rolls all about the yard, while his wife was in the kitchen cooking something good. He threw a few pecks of the rolls onto the roof and laid a few of them just outside the gate as well.

Then he ran into the kitchen shouting, "Woman, you are just like all the others! No sooner do we get a little money in our pockets than you let the housekeeping float off into the blue! The good Lord let it rain bread rolls outside, and you won't even bend over to pick them up!"

"Man, are you stupid?" replied the peasant's wife. "It rained rolls?"

"It certainly did. Go see for yourself," the man replied.

So the peasant woman looked out the window, and when she saw the many thousands of rolls in the yard she was overjoyed. She ran outside, and for the next few hours gathered the rolls, filling three large meat tubs.

When the two weeks had passed, the peasant and his wife were summoned to court. The peasant denied everything, but when the judges turned sternly to his wife, she swore by everything good and true that she had told her neighbor the truth.

"Don't believe the woman, my lords," cried the peasant. "She is not all there upstairs!—Tell them, wife, what else happened when I brought home the chest?"

"Don't you remember, father? It was the day before the good Lord let it rain bread rolls!"

The judges shook their heads, and the peasant said, "Am I not right? She is crazy!"

"I am supposed to be crazy?" continued the woman eagerly. "Peasant, you are right!" said the judges. Thus the peasant was out of trouble, and he went back to his village with his wife and she never gossiped again.

Tale-a-Vision

Gossip can be a problem in the workplace. A gossip will always find it difficult to keep a secret, so he'll share it, often getting an assurance that the person he shares it with will not tell anyone else. But, of course, the receiver does tell someone else — and so the gossip spreads. Although each person in the chain might be considered a gossip, the initial blame should fall on whoever first breaches confidence and tells someone else, whether it's a person telling one's spouse, a spouse telling a friend or relative, or an office worker telling a trusted buddy. The problem is that each person in the chain thinks that he or she can just tell one person who will keep that confidence. But then that person thinks the same way, and so the gossip spreads through the chain of human connections. The result can be devastating. However, as we found in this tale, a little creativity may get the gossip off the hook.

The workplace parallel is the person who wants to pass on some juicy confidential information. A key reason may be to gain power, recognition, or a greater sense of belonging. So, typically, the gossip is a lower-level employee. Managers, supervisors, and executives already have the power, so there is usually no need for them to share someone else's secret. In fact, they would normally not want to share a secret with the employees they manage, since knowing that secret—and keeping it from the higher-ups in the organization—might undermine their own power. By contrast, when lower-level employees share gossip and show off what they know, it's a way of gaining a leg up on their peers At the same time, these other employees can use the information they gain against the person who shouldn't have shared it in the first place. They can let others know they have this information, thereby improving their own status; or they can act on this information, possibly to the detriment of the company (and eventually to the detriment of themselves if the gossip can be traced back to them). Some possible negative consequences are that the company gives up a competitive advantage if the information becomes known to competitors or to the general public before it is ready to be released, or the company might even be exposed to a lawsuit because of the damage the gossip caused. Maybe some gossips could avoid the negative consequences by being clever like the peasant. But often there is no way out: The person is held accountable for the consequences of telling, and so justice is done.

Take That—What to Do

What should you do if you encounter an office gossip, especially if you lack the authority to "put a lid on it?" Here are some tips. Choose and adapt whatever works best in your own work situation:

- If you believe someone is likely to gossip, don't tell that person anything that you don't want shared with others, since the gossip is probably going to do just that.

- Tell the gossip you don't want to hear anything that the gossip claims is secret information; explain that you are afraid you will slip and tell someone else by mistake. Maybe the gossip will get the hint. Talk to the gossip and tell her that she is getting a bad reputation as someone who can't be trusted with private information, because everyone knows she'll tell it to others. Since a main reason most gossips gossip is to impress others and find social acceptance, realizing that the gossip is having the opposite effect may shut some gossips down.

- Have a group meeting where everyone confronts the gossip. Hopefully she'll realize she has been exposed and no longer can be trusted. This may also result in her shutting off the gossip valve.

- Send the gossip an anonymous memo letting her know she has been spreading confidential information to others. This is likely to unnerve her, and she'll stop sharing secrets.

Jack and His Master

(Celtic)

A poor woman had three sons. Two were clever fellows, but they called the youngest one "Jack the Fool" because they thought he was no better than a simpleton. The eldest son got tired of staying at home, and said he'd go look for service. He stayed away a whole year.

When he returned, he told them how he had worked for Brian Finnigan, and that the agreement was, whoever first said he was sorry for making the bargain to work for Finnegan would get an inch of skin taken from his back, from shoulder to hips. If it was the master, he would pay double wages; if it was the servant, he would get no wages at all. "But Brian gave me so little to eat, and kept me so hard at work, that I couldn't stand it. Once when he asked me if I was sorry for my bargain, I was mad enough to say I was, and here I am disabled for life."

The second eldest son said he'd go and take service with Brian Finnigan. "Oh, won't I be glad to see the skin coming off Brian's back," he said. He started off and twelve months later he was back, just as miserable and helpless as his brother.

However, nothing his mother said could prevent Jack the Fool from going to work for Brian Finnigan.

"Now, Jack," said Brian, "if you refuse to do anything you are able to do, you must lose a month's wages."

"I'm satisfied," said Jack, "and if you stop me from doing a thing after telling me to do it, you are to give me an additional month's wages. Or if you blame me for obeying your orders, you must give the same."

"I am satisfied," said the master.

The first day that Jack served he was fed very poorly and was worked very hard. The next day he came in just before dinner. As they were taking the goose off the spit, Jack whipped a knife off the dresser and cut off some meat and began to eat it. In came the master, and began to abuse him. "Oh, you know, master, you're to feed me. Are you sorry for our agreement?"

The master was going to scream at him, but he bethought himself in time. "Oh no, not at all," said he.

Next day Jack was to go clamp turf on the bog. They weren't sorry to have him away from the kitchen at dinner time. Jack's breakfast was not satisfying; so he said to the mistress, "I think, ma'am, it will be better for me to get my lunch now, and not lose time coming home from the bog."

"That's true, Jack," said she. So she brought out a good cake, a pint of butter, and a bottle of milk, thinking he'd take them away to the bog. But Jack kept his seat.

"Now, mistress," said he, "I'll be earlier at my work tomorrow if I sleep comfortably on the side of a pile of dry peat on dry grass. So you may as well give me my supper, and be done with the day's trouble." She gave him supper, thinking he'd take it to the bog. But he ate all the food, and the mistress was astonished.

He spoke to his master and said, "What are servants asked to do in this country after eating their supper?"

"Nothing at all, but to go to bed."

"Oh, very well, sir." He went up on the stable-loft, stripped, and lay down. Someone saw him and told the master."

"Jack, you scoundrel, what are you doing?"

"Sleeping, master. The mistress, God bless her, gave me my

breakfast, lunch, and supper. You told me that bed was the next thing. Do you blame me, sir?"

"Yes, I do."

"Hand me out one pound thirteen and fourpence, if you please, sir. Oh, I see, you've forgotten your bargain. Are you sorry for it?"

"NO! I'll give you the money after your nap."

The next morning Jack asked how he'd be employed that day. The master bade him to go and mind the cows in a field that had half of it under young corn. "Be sure, particularly, to keep Browney away from the wheat," he said. "While she's out of mischief there's no fear of the rest."

About noon, he went to see how Jack was doing his duty, and what did he find but Jack asleep with his face to the sod; Browney grazing near a thorn-tree, one end of a long rope round her horns and the other end round the tree; and the rest of the cows all trampling and eating the green wheat.

"Jack, you vagabond, do you see what the cows are doing?"

"And do you blame me, master?"

"To be sure, you lazy sluggard, I do."

"Hand me out one pound thirteen and fourpence, master. You said if I only kept Browney out of mischief, the rest would do no harm. There she is, as harmless as a lamb. Are you sorry for hiring me, master?"

"I'll give you your money when you go to dinner. Now, understand me; don't let a cow go out of the field nor into the wheat the rest of the day."

"Never fear, master!"

But Brian wished he had not hired him.

The next day three heifers were missing, and the master bade Jack go in search of them.

"Where will I look for them?" said Jack.

"Every place likely and unlikely."

Brian was getting very exact in his words. When he came home at dinner-time, he found Jack pulling armfuls of thatch off the roof.

"What are you doing?"

"I'm looking for the heifers."

"What would bring them there?"

"I don't think anything could bring them there; but I looked in the likely places and now I'm looking in the unlikeliest places. Maybe this is not pleasing to you."

"Sorrow on me that ever I had the bad luck to meet with you."

"You're all witness," said Jack, "that my master says he is sorry for hiring me. My time is up. Master, hand me over double wages, and come into the next room, and lay yourself out like a man that has some decency in him, till I take a strip of skin an inch broad from your shoulder to your hip."

Every one shouted out against that, but Jack said, "You didn't hinder him when he took the same strips from the backs of my two brothers."

"Now, you cruel old villain," said Jack, giving the knife a couple of scrapes along the floor, "I'll make you an offer. Give me, along with my double wages, two hundred guineas to support my poor brothers, and I'll do without the strap."

"No!" said Brian, "I'd let you skin me from head to foot first."

"Here goes then," said Jack with a grin.

Brian roared, "Stop! I'll give the money."

Tale-a-Vision

From one perspective, this fable is about using creativity and initiative to undercut a bad bargain with an unfair employer—and come out ahead. For example, let's say an employee takes a job at a workplace where, as she only found out after accepting the job, her boss cajoles her into working late every evening—with no overtime pay! She might use her wits to conjure a new excuse night after night until the boss finally threatens to fire her. But she's ready for him: Having documented his threats, she contacts a lawyer and threatens the boss with an overtime-pay lawsuit if he doesn't drop his unreasonable demands.

From another perspective, setting aside the master/bully character for a moment, the story illustrates what might happen when an employee fails to follow instructions, constantly makes mistakes, and defends those errors by claiming he was just following the rules. While following the letter rather than the spirit of the rules may show a lack of common sense, it may also be how the employee prevails in a wrongful termination lawsuit.

In either case, there is a bad bargain—for the employee who feels she is being exploited or for the employer who feels an employee is "hiding behind the rules."

Take That—What to Do

What should you do if you feel you have entered into a bad bargain as an employee with an exploitive boss, or as a boss with a worker who uses her wits to get away with flouting the rules? Here are some tips. Choose and adapt whatever works best in your own work situation:

As the employee with an exploitive boss:

- Rather than playing games and tricking the employer by acting lazy or making intentional "mistakes" (which can escalate a conflict with your boss and get you into trouble), try standing up for yourself. Point out to the boss what's unfair and see whether you can renegotiate the agreement. If not, be prepared to walk away. Or, if you have a justified claim, pursue it with the HR department and/or contact a lawyer.

- If you think the employer is offering you a bad agreement, where you will be working under exploitive conditions, don't take the job in the first place — or try to renegotiate the agreement so you have more favorable terms. And if you can't, start looking for a better job with better terms.

As the boss with a difficult employee who hides behind the rules:

- Hold the person accountable, and don't let her set the terms of the agreement. You're the boss and the employee works for you. Don't penalize yourself if the employee doesn't perform the assigned tasks and tries to get out of it by claiming she was only following the rules, when in fact, she was not using common sense in carrying them out.

- Don't enter into an agreement with any employee where you give up your own authority to terminate the agreement if the employee doesn't carry out the expected tasks.

CHAPTER 7

Snakes and Other Overly Defensive Beasts

Introduction

O verly-defensive individuals can be difficult to work with. Whatever you do, you fear they will lash out, sometimes unreasonably and emotionally. It may be tempting to lie to such a person so as not to provoke their wrath, but if they get wind of the lie, the consequences could be disastrous.

Sometimes people act in a threatening manner to cover up their own feelings of powerlessness. Sometimes they're afraid that something they want to hide will be exposed. Whatever the reason, they're defensive about protecting themselves or overly determined to show others they can do something—even when it is not something they can or should do. One example is the boss who will brook no disagreement. Should anyone question him about his decisions, he takes it as an affront to his authority. Another example is the employee who is secretive and defensive about the work he is doing. Sometimes people are like this because they're afraid someone will challenge their productivity, skills, or talents.

What should you do when dealing with either a boss or another employee who behaves in this overly defensive way? The following stories will give you some insights into the many types of overly defensive people you may encounter — and what to do about them.

The Snake and the Holy Man

(India)

Once there was a snake with a rather bad attitude. The small village near where the snake lived was very fearful of this snake. You see, this snake slithered through the grass, silently seeking its victims, and without warning would strike and devour its prey. It was known to eat hens, dogs, and even big animals, like cows. However, what was most upsetting to the villagers was that the snake was even eating their children.

The villagers wanted to be respectful toward all creatures, but this snake had simply gone too far. They knew that something had to be done, and they came together to get something done. The villagers gathered at the edge of the field, and with drumming and shouting, with sticks and stones, and with their minds made up they started their search to find the snake and to kill it.

A holy man came upon this loud and angry crowd and asked, "What is this about?"

The villagers told him of the snake's evilness and how the snake was even eating their children. The holy man asked, "If I make this snake stop, and it no longer eats your children, and hunts your farm animals, will you spare the snake's life?"

The villagers argued among themselves. Some wanted vengeance and others were willing to let the holy man try. Most of the villagers did not believe that the holy man would succeed and keep the snake from biting. However, reluctantly, they all agreed to give the snake one chance.

The holy man entered the field and commanded the snake

to come to him. And the power of the holy man caused the snake to crawl to the path and to the feet of the holy man.

"What issss it?" the snake hissed.

The holy man's words were simple: "Enough! There is no need for this. There is plenty of food without eating the village children or their animals."

Now it was not so much what the holy man said, but how he said it. There was a kindness and an authority in the holy man's voice. The snake knew the holy man's words to be true. The snake did not hiss a word but nodded in agreement and slithered away.

It was not long before the villagers discovered that the snake would not harm them. They were grateful that the snake no longer would bite. However, some of the villagers in their anger and hurt from what the snake had done and some in their meanness began to beat the snake with sticks and stones. Day after day the snake received more and more abuse until it could take no more and it hid underneath a large rock.

The snake hid underneath that rock, determined not to break its word to the holy man. However, it was very confused and said to itself, "Why is this happening to me? I listened and followed the holy man's words." The snake was so fearful of leaving its hiding place that it was soon dying from the villagers' beatings and the lack of food.

One day, the weakened snake heard the footsteps of the holy man, and with every bit of strength it crawled out to meet him on the path. The holy man, seeing how terribly beaten and sickly the snake looked, asked, "What has happened to you?"

The snake with great effort told the story of the beatings and torment that it received from the villagers, and how for days it had hidden underneath a rock to protect itself.

The holy man stood silently shaking his head. His voice was low as he said, "Oh, foolish snake, I told you not to bite but I did not say anything about hissing."

And with this the snake understood and slithered away hissing.

Tale-a-Vision

In this case, the snake is an example of the person who has developed a protective "skin" because he is afraid of being hurt. Just like the snake, when he perceives a threat he hisses and threatens, and keeps others at a distance. If they don't keep their distance, the "snake" may actually bite — or simply retreat and hide under a rock, He doesn't want others to get too close, fearful of what they might do. Yet, if you can get behind that barrier, if you can show him you can be trusted, he may begin to feel as though he can shed his protective skin.

You probably know people like this. For instance, when you ask a coworker a few questions about a report she is working on, and she goes on the defensive, asking, "Why do you want to know?" Or you might want to help a coworker who is struggling to complete a task, but immediately, fearing his own authority might be threatened, he reacts defensively by telling you curtly: "No, I don't need any help," or "That's okay. I have it all under control." So you back off. You may have observed a boss acting this way after making a presentation, then either refusing to answer any questions or shooting them down without taking them seriously. Another "snake strategy" is to put others down with biting words and stinging insults — in other words, building oneself up at the expense of others.

Take That—What to Do?

What should you do when you encounter such a defensive person? What do you do when you don't have the authority to challenge someone in authority yourself? Here are some tips. Choose and adapt whatever works best in your own work situation:

- Take some time to get to know the individual. Be kind and helpful; show you can be trusted. For example, share some helpful information with that person, without expecting anything back in return. He may very well shed his protective skin.

- Approach the individual lowly and cautiously; don't get too close or he may feel defensive and put up his guard. For example, keep conversations short and to the point at first, and get to know him gradually.

- Realize that the person may be shy and uncomfortable around people, and give him the space to come out and relate to others on his own terms. Don't try to force a relationship beyond the individual's comfortable level.

- Find ways to show that you and others mean no harm. For example, invite the individual out to lunch, or an after-work gathering, with a group of people from the office. Keep it casual, so he feels he can drop in or out as he pleases. Then, gradually, he may feel less threatened and more comfortable.

• If your boss is the snake, just keep your distance and be especially respectful. You don't want her to feel like you put her on the spot or cornered her, which may lead her to get angry or strike back.

The Emperor Trojan's Goat's Ears

(Serbia)

Once upon a time there lived an emperor whose name was Trojan, and he had ears like a goat. Every morning, when he was shaved, he asked whether the barber saw anything odd about him. When each fresh barber always replied that the emperor had goat's ears, he was at once ordered to be put to death.

Now after this state of things had lasted a good while, there was hardly a barber left in the town who could shave the emperor, and it came to be the turn of the Master of the Company of Barbers to go up to the palace. But, unluckily, at the very moment that he should have set out, the master fell suddenly ill, and he told one of his apprentices that he must go in his stead.

When the youth was taken to the emperor's bedroom, he was asked why he had come and not his master. The young man replied that the master was ill, and there was no one but himself who could be trusted with the honor. The emperor was satisfied with the answer, and sat down, and let a sheet of fine linen be put round him.

Directly the young barber began his work. Like the others before him, he noticed the goat's ears of the emperor, but when he had finished and the emperor asked his usual question as to whether the youth had noticed anything odd about him, the young man replied calmly, "No, nothing at all."

This pleased the emperor so much that he gave him twelve ducats, and said, "Henceforth you shall come every day to shave me."

So when the apprentice returned home, and the master inquired how he had got on with the emperor, the young man answered, "Oh, very well. And he says I am to shave him every day, and he has given me these twelve ducats." But he said nothing about the emperor's goat's ears.

From this time on, the apprentice went regularly up to the palace, receiving each morning twelve ducats in payment. But after a while, his secret, which he had carefully kept, burned within him, and he longed to tell it to somebody. His master saw there was something on his mind, and asked what it was. The youth replied that he had been tormenting himself for some months, and should never feel easy until some one shared his secret.

"Well, trust me," said the master, "I will keep it to myself; or, if you do not like to do that, confess it to your pastor, or go into some field outside the town and dig a hole, and, after you have dug it, kneel down and whisper your secret three times into the hole. Then put back the earth and come away."

The apprentice thought that this seemed the best plan, and that very afternoon went to a meadow outside the town, dug a deep hole, then knelt and whispered into it three times over, "The Emperor Trojan has goat's ears." And as he said so a great burden seemed to roll off him, and he shoveled the earth carefully back and ran lightly home.

Weeks passed away, and there sprang up in the hole an elder tree, which had three stems, all as straight as poplars. Some shepherds, tending their flocks near by, noticed the tree growing there. One of them cut down a stem from which to make flutes. But as soon as he began to play, the flute would do nothing but sing, "The Emperor Trojan has goat's ears." Of course, it was not long before the whole town knew of this wonderful flute and what it said, and soon the news reached the emperor in his palace.

He instantly sent for the apprentice and said to him, "What have you been saying about me to all my people?"

The culprit tried to defend himself by saying that he had never told anyone what he had noticed, but the emperor, instead of listening, only drew his sword from its sheath. This so frightened the poor fellow that he confessed exactly what he had done, and how he had whispered the truth three times to the earth, and how in that very place an elder tree had sprung up, and flutes had been cut from it, which would only repeat the words he had said.

Then the emperor commanded his coach to be made ready, and he took the youth with him, and they drove to the spot, for he wished to see for himself whether the young man's confession was true. But when they reached the place, only one stem was left. So the emperor desired his attendants to cut him a flute from the remaining stem, and, when it was ready, he ordered his chamberlain to play on it. But no tune could the chamberlain play, though he was the best flute player about the court. Nothing came out but the words, "The Emperor Trojan has goat's ears."

Then the emperor knew that even the earth gave up its secrets, and he granted the young man his life, but he didn't allow him to be his barber anymore.

Tale-a-Vision

This is an example of someone who is very sensitive about a personal flaw. Such individuals will go to incredible lengths to cover up. They don't want anyone knowing about, discussing, or drawing attention to that flaw.

Such flaws can take various forms. A once heavy-set woman doesn't want others to know about her weight-reduction surgery; she'd rather her office mates think she lost weight as a result of her own willpower. A salesman wants to conceal his plastic surgery to appear more youthful, so he will seem more dynamic and successful. A boss doesn't want to reveal his lack of knowledge about using the Internet, so he hires someone in the office to do some searching for him and then passes off the successful results as his own, while the employee who did the work is not permitted to say anything.

In this tale, such efforts to conceal drive the Emperor Trojan. He doesn't want anyone to know that he has the ears of a goat, which is considered just a lowly farm animal.

A modern office parallel is the revelation of the boss's or manager's embarrassing secret. Perhaps he wears a toupee or dyes his hair out of vanity; perhaps he was arrested for drunk driving. As long as the boss thinks that just one person knows the secret, he can easily threaten that person with consequences for ratting him out, such as being fired, being kept from a promotion, or being transferred to an undesirable position in the company. But once the truth comes out, like the earth giving up its secrets, the boss may not be able to do anything about it. He can't fire, fail to promote, or transfer everyone without damaging the company, so he just has to live with everyone knowing his secret.

Take That—What to Do

What should you do when you know a boss's or coworker's secret—especially if you're uncomfortable keeping it? Here are some tips. Choose and adapt whatever works best in your own work situation:

- As long as this is just an embarrassing secret—not one involving something illegal—keep the secret, and don't feel guilty about that. Why embarrass another person unnecessarily? There's no need to "tell the earth."

- If you do feel an overpowering need to spill the beans, at least don't let it get back to others in the office. For example, tell someone you trust, but change names and identifying details, so if that person slips up, others will not know who it is about.

- Help to reassure the person there is no need to keep the secret, because it is not as embarrassing or demeaning as he thinks. Let him know that others will understand and appreciate him for his candor.

Tale #21:

The Wicked Prince

(Denmark)

Once upon a time there was a proud and wicked prince, who thought only about how he might conquer all the nations of the earth and make his name a terror to all mankind. He plunged forth with fire and sword. His soldiers trampled down the grain in the fields, and they put the torch to the peasants' cottages so that the red flames licked the very leaves from the trees, and the fruit hung roasted from black and charred limbs. Many a poor mother caught up her naked baby and tried to hide behind the smoking walls, but the soldiers followed her, and if they found her and the child, then began their devilish pleasure. Evil spirits could do no worse, but the prince rejoiced in it all.

Day by day his power increased; his name was feared by all, and fortune followed him in all his deeds. From the conquered cities he carried away gold and precious treasures, until he had amassed in his capital riches such as were unequaled in any other place. Then he built superb palaces and temples and arches, and whoever saw his magnificence said, "What a great prince!" Never did they think of the misery he had brought upon other lands; never did they listen to the groans and lamentations from cities laid waste by fire.

The prince gazed upon his gold, looked at his superb buildings, and thought like the crowd, "What a great prince!" But he added, "I must have more, much more! There is no power that can equal — much less surpass — mine!" And so he warred with his neighbors until all were defeated. The conquered kings were chained to his chariot with chains of gold when he drove through the streets; and when he sat at table they lay at the feet of the prince and his courtiers, eating such scraps as might be thrown to them.

Now the prince had his own statue set up in the market places and the palaces; yes, he would even have set it in the churches, on the altars, but to this the priests said, "Prince, you are great, but God is greater! We dare not obey your orders!"

"Well," said the evil prince, "then I shall conquer God, too!" In the pride and folly of his heart he had built a splendidly constructed ship, in which he could sail through the air. It was as colorful as a peacock's tail, and seemed decorated with a thousand eyes, but each eye was the barrel of a cannon. The prince could sit in the center of the ship and, upon his touching a certain button, a thousand bullets would stream forth, and the guns would at once be reloaded. Hundreds of strong eagles were harnessed to the ship, and so it flew away, up and up toward the sun.

Far beneath lay the earth. At first its mountains and forests appeared like a plowed field, with a tuft of green peeping out here and there from the sod; then it seemed like an unrolled map; and finally it was wholly hidden in mists and clouds, as the eagles flew higher and higher.

Then God sent forth a single one of His countless angels, and immediately the prince let fly a thousand bullets at him, but they bounced back like hail from the angel's shining wings. Then one drop of blood — just one — fell from one of the angel's white wing feathers onto the ship of the prince. There it burned itself into it, and its weight of a thousand hundredweights of lead hurled the ship back down with terrible speed to the earth. The mighty wings of the eagles were broken, the winds roared about the head of the prince, and the clouds on every side, sprung from the smoke of burned cities, formed themselves into menacing shapes. Some were like mile-long crabs stretching out their huge claws toward him; others were like tumbling boulders or fire-breathing dragons. The prince lay half dead in his ship, until it was finally caught in the tangled branches of a dense forest.

"I *will* conquer God!" he said. "I have sworn it; my will shall be done!" Then for seven years he built other magnificent ships in which to sail through the air, and had lightning beams forged from the hardest of steels, to batter down the battlements of heaven itself. From all the conquered countries he assembled vast armies which, when formed in battle array, covered mile after mile of ground.

They embarked in the magnificent ships, but as the prince approached his own, God sent forth a swarm of gnats — just one little swarm — which buzzed about the prince, and stung his face and hands. In rage he drew his sword, but he could cut only the empty air; he could not strike the gnats. Then he ordered that he be brought costly cloths, which were to be wrapped around him so that no gnat could reach him with its sting. His orders were carried out; but one little gnat had concealed itself in the innermost covering, and now it crept into the prince's ear and stung him. It smarted like fire, and the poison rushed into his brain; he tore the clothes loose and flung them far away from him, rent his garments into rags, and danced naked before the rugged and savage soldiers. Now they could only mock at the mad prince who had started out to conquer God and had been himself conquered by a single little gnat!

Tale-a-Vision

In this case, the difficult person is someone who is so prideful and power-hungry that he repeatedly outreaches himself and doesn't let others dissuade him. This is someone who wants to take down the competition and who enjoys destroying others. He likes being feared, and initially may be very successful, while creating a swath of ruin as he amasses more and more power and money. The devastation caused to others is unimportant; only his own aggrandizement matters. Eventually he tries to do more than is humanly possible — and fails.

The parallel here is the boss who is determined to take on the competition or who so enjoys putting down others that she becomes reckless. For example, the company owner is so intent on outspending a competitor that she fails to see how these efforts are undermining her own company's bottom line. Another example is the person who enjoys putting others down and revels in their destruction, such as the boss who continually belittles her employees. While the tyrant may enjoy some great success, particularly if she is considered brilliant in a highly competitive field, she may go too far and be brought down by, say, a discrimination lawsuit or having a strategic mistake exposed.

Take That—What to Do

What should you do when you are confronted by a person who comes on like one of these people — eager to show off their power and conquer all, regardless of the consequences for others? What do you do when you don't have the authority to challenge someone in authority yourself? Here are some tips from which you can choose and adapt whatever works best to your own work situation.

- Quietly wait it out and go along, as long as it is to your advantage to stay in the company. Eventually, the person is likely to self-destruct.

- Discreetly let others know what the difficult person is doing, so gradually the word spreads, and others react by resisting or further spreading the word, which will eventually result in the difficult person's overthrow.

- Join together with other employees who have been similarly mistreated. If you can't confront the boss directly, take it upstairs to the boss's boss or human resources, or take it outside to a lawyer.

- If you think the individual may be doing something illegal to consolidate power and you have no other recourse, consider going to a government agency and letting them know what's happening.

CHAPTER 8

Monkeys and Other Insincere, Poorly Communicating Beasts

Introduction

Communication can be a problem in any workplace. When people don't communicate clearly, the receiver gets the wrong message. Sometimes, because people aren't sure how their message will be received, they prefer to communicate nothing. In other cases, people exaggerate or lie to appear a certain way, to convince others of their point of view, or to manipulate others into doing what they want. And many people simply misunderstand or don't want to hear a message that seems unfavorable to them, and so they misinterpret or deny. Then, too, a communication may mean one thing to one person and something else to another, even though what was spoken and what was heard were the same. Or messages may get garbled in transmission, so that only part of the message gets through, creating confusion and misunderstandings.

Surely, you can think of numerous other ways in which people don't communicate well or do so to manipulate. It is a very common reason that things don't go well in the workplace. As the acronym SNAFU—a military abbreviation used in World War II meaning "situation normal, all fouled up"—implies, the communication means to instruct, guide, inform, clarify, or otherwise impart knowledge, but instead it does just the opposite. So the communication is misrepresented or not received at all. Even when it is received, it misleads, because it conceals the communicator's real agenda.

So what kinds of miscommunications occur in your office—or with others you know? What should you do to improve your communications? And how do you recognize when someone is trying to manipulate you into doing something that would be harmful for you? The following stories will give you some insights into the many types of miscommunications that occur and what to do to protect yourself from unfortunate outcomes.

The Quarrel of the Monkey and the Crab

(Japan)

Long, long ago, one bright autumn day in Japan, it happened that a pink-faced monkey and a yellow crab were playing together along the bank of a river. As they were running about, the crab found a rice-dumpling and the monkey a persimmon seed.

The crab picked up the rice-dumpling and showed it to the monkey, saying:

"Look what a nice thing I have found!"

Then the monkey held up his persimmon seed and said:

"I also have found something good! Look!"

Now though the monkey is always very fond of persimmon fruit, he had no use for the seed he had just found. The persimmon seed is as hard and uneatable as a stone. Therefore, because of his greedy nature, the monkey felt very envious of the crab's nice dumpling, and he proposed an exchange. The crab naturally did not see why he should give up his prize for a hard stone-like seed, and would not consent to the monkey's proposition.

Then the cunning monkey began to persuade the crab, saying:

"How unwise you are not to think of the future! Your rice-dumpling can be eaten now, and is certainly much bigger than my seed; but if you sow this seed in the ground it will soon grow and become a great tree in a few years, and bear an abundance of fine ripe persimmons year after year. If only I could show it to you then, with the yellow fruit hanging on its

branches! Of course, if you don't believe me I shall sow it myself; though I am sure, later on, you will be very sorry that you
did not take my advice."

The simple-minded crab could not resist the monkey's
clever persuasion. He at last gave in and consented to the monkey's proposal, and the exchange was made. The greedy monkey soon gobbled up the dumpling, and with great reluctance
gave up the persimmon seed to the crab. He would have liked
to keep that too, but he was afraid of making the crab angry
and of being pinched by his sharp scissor-like claws. They
then separated, the monkey going home to his forest trees and
the crab to his stones along the river-side. As soon as the crab
reached home he put the persimmon seed in the ground as the
monkey had told him.

In the following spring the crab was delighted to see the
shoot of a young tree push its way up through the ground. Each
year it grew bigger, till at last it blossomed one spring, and in the
following autumn bore some fine large persimmons. Among
the broad smooth green leaves the fruit hung like golden balls,
and as they ripened they mellowed to a deep orange. It was
the little crab's pleasure to go out day by day and sit in the sun
and put out his long eyes in the same way as a snail puts out its
horn, and watch the persimmons ripening to perfection.

"How delicious they will be to eat!" he said to himself.

At last, one day, he knew the persimmons must be quite
ripe and he wanted very much to taste one. He made several at-
tempts to climb the tree, in the vain hope of reaching one of the
beautiful persimmons hanging above him; but he failed each
time, for a crab's legs are not made for climbing trees but only
for running along the ground and over stones, both of which

he can do most cleverly. In his dilemma he thought of his old playmate the monkey, who, he knew, could climb trees better than any one else in the world. He determined to ask the monkey to help him, and set out to find him.

Running crab-fashion up the stony river bank, over the pathways into the shadowy forest, the crab at last found the monkey taking an afternoon nap in his favorite pine-tree, with his tail curled tight around a branch to prevent him from falling off in his sleep. He was soon wide awake, however, when he heard himself called, and eagerly listening to what the crab told him. When he heard that the seed which he had long ago exchanged for a rice-dumpling had grown into a tree and was now bearing good fruit, he was delighted, for he at once devised a cunning plan which would give him all the persimmons for himself.

He consented to go with the crab to pick the fruit for him. When they both reached the spot, the monkey was astonished to see what a fine tree had sprung from the seed, and with what a number of ripe persimmons the branches were loaded.

He quickly climbed the tree and began to pluck and eat, as fast as he could, one persimmon after another. Each time he chose the best and ripest he could find, and went on eating till he could eat no more. Not one did he give to the poor hungry crab waiting below, and when he had finished there was little left but the hard, unripe fruit.

You can imagine the feelings of the poor crab — after he had waited patiently so long for the tree to grow and the fruit to ripen — when he saw the monkey devouring all the good persimmons. He was so disappointed that he ran round and round the tree calling to the monkey to remember his promise. The monkey at first took no notice of the crab's complaints, but at last he picked out the hardest, greenest persimmon he could find and aimed it at the crab's head. The persimmon is as hard as stone when it is unripe. The monkey's missile struck home and the crab was sorely hurt by the blow. Again and again, as fast as he could pick them, the monkey pulled off the hard persimmons and threw them at the defenseless crab till he dropped dead, covered with wounds all over his body. There he lay, a pitiful sight at the foot of the tree he had himself planted.

When the wicked monkey saw that he had killed the crab he ran away from the spot as fast as he could, in fear and trembling, like the coward he was.

Tale-a-Vision

The manipulative communicator can be especially dangerous. He seems so sincere that you go along, never realizing that you are falling into a dangerous trap. Sometimes manipulative communicators are so persuasive that they can make you forget the old adage that if something seems too good to be true, it probably isn't true.

That's what happened to the crab in a story. He got pulled into a deadly trap by believing the conniving monkey. Malicious communicators can create visions of what is possible, while concealing a hidden agenda. As a result, the person who listens can become a victim, who not only doesn't get what is promised, but can be destroyed, just like the crab, who believed unwisely in the monkey's words. For example, there are unscrupulous people who manipulate others into financial schemes that dupe investors. It may be easy to push away such schemes when you are approached by someone you don't know, so you may be readily suspicious. But you can easily be sucked in when it's someone at work, whom you have come to know and trust, such as a coworker or boss.

One person tells you about something he is doing on the side and makes it seem like such a good deal that you invest. Another person talks you into doing a job you don't want to do with a promise of a great new promotion or job opportunity at the end. Then you find that you have taken on a dead-end assignment, and have been pushed out of the way for the plum job that the manipulator wanted — and got.

Take That—What to Do

So what do you do when someone offers you a seemingly great opportunity that makes it seem like you are getting the better of the deal or that seems too good to be true? How do you know when to believe the person and agree to do whatever she wants you to do, and when to recognize that you may be walking into a dangerous trap? Here are some tips. Choose and adapt whatever works best in your own work situation:

- Ask more questions about what the person is offering, so you have a very clear picture of the offer. If possible, get it documented so you can see whether what the person says is supported by what's in writing. If it isn't, don't trust the deal.

- If someone is offering you what seems like the better deal and taking less himself, ask yourself why he should be doing that. Generally, no one wants to get the short end of the stick in any exchange, so there may be a catch. Look for that, so you won't find yourself caught in a trap.

- Look for any hidden agendas or messages when someone who is a very compelling and persuasive communicator tries to convince you of something. Take some time to check out what the person is saying before you decide to take the deal. Think of a used-car salesman, who may or may not be offering you a good deal. Look beneath the surface words to make sure you're not getting stuck with a lemon.

- Consider your own limitations when you enter into any agreement, so you don't enter into a situation where your limitations will prevent you from being successful, like the crab, which wasn't able to climb a tree himself and had to turn to the monkey for help.

- Recognize whether the deal is a first step toward a situation where you will need help from the person bringing you into the deal. Don't be like the person who goes to a free lecture, only to find she is drawn into a series of very expensive workshops that promise great success in the distant future.

Tale #23:

The Little Boy Who Talked with Birds

(Mayan)

Some say that birds speak with each other in their own language and that this language is universal and full of harmonies that have no equal in the world. Among the Mayans who lived long ago there were people who could understand clearly those messages of the birds and who enjoyed immensely their beautiful dialogues and all the words they sang. Sometimes they were quick to heed the prophecies they heard. Sometimes the birds only sang, but other times their notes were messages for passers-by.

So it was with the young worker who went with his father to work in the fields every day. He never complained, even when his father treated him badly. On the contrary, like any decent boy he loved and respected his parents. When lunchtime came, the father and his son would sit in the shade of a tree beside the fields and drink the grain soup and eat their tortillas with beans and wild greens. At this hour a beautiful bird also arrived and perched in the tree above them. Each day he sang in the same way.

After listening intently to the bird's song, the boy would laugh, or sometimes only smile so his father would not notice his odd behavior. This happened every day he went to work in the cornfield. Whenever the bird began to sing, the boy would laugh, trying not to annoy his father.

One day, however, the father asked gruffly, "What is it saying, this bird that comes to sing to us?"

"It just feels like singing," the boy answered.

"And why do you laugh when it sings, if it is only singing?"

"Only because I enjoy hearing it sing, nothing more," the boy said.

"If it pleases you, then it is because it is saying something. Tell me!" the angry father ordered.

"It doesn't say anything," the boy replied casually.

"Don't try to hide it from me. Tell me quickly or I'll give you a beating!" the father warned.

The father's threats grew more severe. Because the boy did not want to anger his father anymore, he said, "Since you insist, I will tell you. It says you will have to salute me one day."

The father felt insulted. "Salute you! Are you crazy?"

"No. It is not I who says it, but the bird."

The father became even angrier and exclaimed, "All right, how is it going to happen that a father salutes a son?"

"I don't know. You insisted and I have only told you what the bird was singing."

The father was very upset by all of this because he thought his son was losing respect for him and that a day would come when the boy would humiliate him. The rigid man began to treat the boy even more unjustly, finally throwing him out of the house.

The boy bore this injustice patiently and wandered aimlessly about the world, like an orphan or a lost child. When he had traveled for a long time, the boy came to the domain of a great chief, where by chance he heard the following proclamation:

He who can interpret the squawks of the crows who come every afternoon fluttering about the chief's window, can marry the chief's daughter and inherit the kingdom.

Many had tried to pass the test, but their interpretations had not satisfied the chief. The proof of this was that the crows kept coming to the window every afternoon to disturb the chief, never heeding any reply to their squawking. Then someone told the chief that a strange boy had arrived in the community, and the chief immediately ordered that he be brought before him.

The boy came before the great chief and asked why he had been called. The chief replied, "Two crows come here every afternoon to flutter about and squawk through my window. Now I am fed up with them. How should I know what they want? Many have tried to understand what these birds say, but they have all failed. Stay here until they come and let's see if you can resolve this problem."

That afternoon the two birds arrived at the usual hour and began to squawk loudly. The boy approached the window and then smiled as he listened to the excited squawking. When they finished, the boy told the chief what he had understood.

"The male crow says that the female crow abandoned her eggs and that he had to keep them warm until the little boy crow and little girl crow hatched. And the female crow says the male crow didn't carry any food to the nest and that's why she disappeared. But now she has reappeared to claim her legitimate children, the two baby crows."

"*Ay, caramba.* And now, now what do we do?" the chief asked.

The boy answered quickly. "Well, the male crow should take the little girl crow and the female should take the little boy crow."

So the boy told this to the crows that very afternoon, and they were immediately satisfied with the solution and flew off happily.

After that, the chief was satisfied, and he soon fulfilled his vow by marrying his daughter to the boy, who soon inherited all that the chief owned. All the people from the neighboring villages attended the wedding feast. Among them came two old people whom the boy soon recognized.

Everyone came forward to salute the new chief, including the old couple. They greeted him respectfully, "Good health to you, great lord!" the trembling old man said.

The young chief rushed forward to greet the old man and said, "Don't bow before me and don't salute me, because I am your son. Don't you remember me and that bird and how you made me tell you what he said in his song?"

"Oh, my son! Forgive me for what I have done to you," the old man sobbed.

The boy embraced his parents and announced, "Don't worry, father. I'm not angry. From today on, you and mother will live near me so our family can be reborn in peace and happiness."

And so, when the prophecy of the bird who sang by the cornfield came to pass, thus ended the story of the boy who understood the language of the birds.

Tale-a-Vision

One of the most common problems in communication occurs when people who don't want to hear unfavorable news reject the message. It's sometimes called "killing the messenger," something kings might have done when they didn't like the battle news that a messenger brought them. But people who do that ultimately find that reality catches up, and whether they like or not, the message is what it is. They are like ostriches who bury their head in the sand, not wanting to face a danger, so they don't escape, and instead suffer the consequences of not facing the looming danger and doing something about it. Or, as in this tale, rejecting a communication can lead to a damaged relationship or fighting back against the messenger with the message, rather than accepting it.

That's what the father did in this story, which parallels a workplace where a supervisor or manager doesn't want to hear a message about something that might undermine her authority — such as how well a particular employee is doing — because she fears that the employee might get too much credit and even endanger her own job. So she tries to squelch the information and starts mistreating the employee delivering that information or the employee doing the good job — just out of resentment and fear.

The result is that these actions can sow anger and disharmony among employees, undermining operations and productivity. This sets a vicious cycle in motion, one where the mistreatment can elicit even poorer performance, leading to further mistreatment or to unjust termination. But the actual problem is the boss's refusal to accept the information she has been given. This is exactly what happened in the folktale, where the father first beats his son and finally kicks him out of the house.

Take That—What to Do

What should you do when you are confronted by a person who doesn't want to listen to an unfavorable message in the workplace — especially if you lack the authority to challenge the individual? Here are some tips. Choose and adapt whatever works best in your own work situation:

- If this is a very important message and your boss or other person doesn't want to listen, maybe she would listen to someone else. To that end, see whether you can share the message with someone else or others you trust — and then let them try to present the message.

- You might be able to get the message across if you present it in a different, more compelling way. For example, if you tried initially to express yourself verbally, try writing up a memo or report where you not only provide the message, but offer supporting facts to make it more persuasive.

- Consider ways to soften the message, so it becomes more acceptable. For example, highlight the benefits or favorable results that will come about as a result of listening to the message.

- If your own supervisor or manager won't listen, maybe you can find someone above her who will. Perhaps you can make that presentation yourself. Or you may need to find someone you trust to contact that person, or send an anonymous memo showing why this message is so important.

- If all else fails, consider quitting because of the expected problems that will occur once the message comes to pass. Or consider quitting anyway, because people aren't listening to you.

Tale #24:

The Most Indispensable Thing

(Germany)

Ages ago there lived a king who had three good and beautiful daughters whom he loved very much and who in turn loved him dearly. He had no princes, but in his kingdom it was the custom that the succession of the throne could also pass to women and daughters. Because the king's wife was no longer alive he was free to appoint one of his daughters to the throne, and it did not need to be the oldest one.

Because this king loved all of his daughters equally, the decision was very difficult for him. He came to the conclusion to select the one who demonstrated the keenest intellect. He shared this determination with his three daughters, declaring that his approaching birthday would be the day of decision. The one who would bring him "the most indispensable thing" would become queen.

Each of the princesses thought about what would be the most indispensable thing. When his birthday arrived, the oldest one approached him, carrying a fine purple robe, and said, "The Lord God had mankind come naked into the world, but then he barred them from paradise. Thus robes and clothing are indispensable."

The second daughter brought a loaf of fresh bread that she herself had baked. It was lying on top of a filled beaker made of gold. "Food and drink are the most indispensable things for mankind, born from dust, for without these we cannot live. Thus God created the fruits of the field, fruit, berries, and grapes, and taught mankind to make bread and wine, the sacred symbols of his love."

The youngest daughter brought a pile of salt on a wooden plate, saying, "My father, I consider salt and wood to be the most indispensable. Ancient peoples paid sacred homage to the trees and considered salt to be holy."

The king was very surprised with these gifts. Thinking about them, he said, "Purple is the most indispensable thing for a king, for if he has it, he has everything else. If he loses it, then he is no longer king and is as common as other humans. Because you have perceived this, my oldest and beloved daughter, after me you shall be decorated with royal purple. Come to me and receive my thanks and my blessing!"

After kissing and blessing his oldest daughter, he said to the second oldest, "Eating and drinking are not altogether necessary, my good child, and they draw us down entirely too much into commonness. They are a sign of mediocrity and of the masses. I cannot hinder you if you find pleasure therein, nor can I thank you for your poorly chosen gift, but you shall be blessed for your good will." Then the king blessed his daughter, but he did not kiss her.

Then he turned to the third princess, who was standing there, pale and trembling. After what she had seen and heard, she sensed what was to come.

"My daughter, on your wooden plate you may well have some salt, but in your brain you have none," said the king. "You are still alive, and therefore salt is not indispensable. One does not need salt. With your salt you are showing the sense of a peasant, not the sense of a king. And I take no pleasure on that stiff wooden thing. Thus I can neither thank you nor bless you.

Go away from me, as far as your feet will carry you. Go to the stupid and coarse people who worship old blocks of wood and tree limbs instead of the living God, and who consider common salt to be sacred."

Crying, the youngest princess then turned away from her hard father, and walked far, far away from the court and the royal city, as far as her feet would carry her. She came to an inn and offered her services to the female innkeeper. The innkeeper was touched by her humility, innocence, youth, and beauty, and she took her in as a maid. The princess soon mastered all the household duties, and the innkeeper said, "It would be a pity if the girl did not learn a decent skill. I'll teach her to cook."

And thus the princess learned to cook. She grasped everything quickly, and soon could cook some dishes even better and more delicious than the teacher herself. Business improved at the inn because of the good cooking there, and the reputation of the good cook — who also happened to be young and beautiful — spread throughout the entire land.

Now it came to pass that her father the king's oldest daughter was about to be married. A royal wedding was to be held, and it was recommended to bring the famous cook to the court to prepare the feast, for the lords at the royal court, the marshals, the royal wine stewards, the royal dining stewards, the masters of ceremony, the chamberlains, and other excellencies did not share the view that their most gracious lord the king had once expressed, that eating and drinking were not altogether necessary and that they draw us down to commonness. To the contrary, they praised all good food and fine wine and honored — at least inwardly — that old and true proverb, *Eating and drinking hold body and soul together*.

The wedding meal was deliciously prepared, including the king's favorite dish, which had been specially ordered by the royal dining steward. The meal was served. There came one dish after the other, and each was highly praised.

Finally came the king's favorite dish, and it was served first to him. He tried it and found it completely tasteless. His cheerful mood darkened, and he spoke to the chamberlain standing behind his golden armchair, "This dish is ruined! It is terrible! Stop the platters from being passed around, and summon the cook!"

The cook entered the magnificent hall, and the king addressed her, "You have ruined my favorite dish. You have spoiled my pleasure by not putting any salt in my favorite dish!"

Then the cook fell at the king's feet, saying with humility, "Have mercy, your majesty, my royal lord, and forgive me! How could I have dared to mix salt into your food? Did I not once hear from a lofty king's own mouth the words, "One does not need salt. Salt is not indispensable. Salt shows only the sense of a peasant, not the sense of a king!"

With shame the king recognized these words as his own and the cook as his daughter. Lifting her from the floor where she was kneeling, he drew her to his heart. He then told all the wedding guests her story and had his youngest daughter once again be seated by his side.

Then the wedding became doubly joyful, and the king was once again entirely happy with his daughter's love.

Tale-a-Vision

Another common communication problem is not valuing other people's insights and contributions. People who are quick to judge and reject risk casting aside truly valuable wisdom and advice.

That's the case in this tale, where a king is trying to decide which daughter will succeed him, based on the gift (the message) she is bringing him. The workplace parallel is the boss who doesn't recognize the meaning or import of a message. This individual is simply clueless and unable to acknowledge that.

For example, let's say it is very important for a boss to approve an upgrade of the technology now in use, authorize the purchase of new equipment, or agree to the restructuring of the roles and responsibilities of people in the office. You try to tell him something needs to be done quickly or the company will start falling behind in productivity or in the appeal of its products in the market, but he ignores your advice. You're up against someone who doesn't know and doesn't know he doesn't know. The message is rejected, not because the person understands the message and doesn't like what it says, but because he simply doesn't understand and acknowledge its value.

Take That—What to Do

What should you do when you are confronted by a person who doesn't know and doesn't know he doesn't know? How can you get such an individual to accept valuable information? Here are some tips. Choose and adapt whatever works best in your own work situation:

- If you can't convince the person yourself, try asking others for help. Maybe another person can speak the language this person will understand, or maybe you'll find powers in numbers, so the group may be able to convince the person to recognize the value of this information.

- If you can't show why your message is important by explaining it one way, try another way. For example, instead of presenting this information in person, try sending a written memo or report that may be more persuasive.

- Look for an opportunity to demonstrate why your information is correct and should be heeded. For example, if you see an article supporting your point of view, clip it and find an opportunity to show it to the person.

- Tell others in the organization about your ideas. As others start talking, the person you want to convince may hear the favorable opinions of others and come around.

- Go to someone in higher authority in the organization and tell them your ideas by setting up a meeting or sending a memo. Be diplomatic: Explain that you are just trying to help the company, not trying to portray the other person as someone who doesn't understand.

Index

About the Authors

Terrence L. Gargiulo is President of MakingStories.net and one of the leading authorities on the use of stories and narrative in business situations. He is the author of *On Cloud Nine: Weathering the Challenge of Many Generations in the Workplace,* among many other titles, and lives in Monterey, California. He can be reached at terrence@makingstories.net; his website is www.makingstories.net. **Gini Graham Scott**, Ph.D., is the founder and director of Changemakers and the author of many books about the workplace, including *Disagreements, Disputes, and All-Out War; A Survival Guide for Working with Humans*; and *A Survival Guide for Working with Bad Bosses.* She lives in Oakland and Santa Monica, California. Her website is www.ginigrahamscott.com; the website for her books is www.workingwithhumans.com. **Ron Dias** has been an artist illustrating books and working on films for Disney for the past fifty years. He resides in Monterey, California.